Edward Dennett

Fundamental Truths of Salvation

Being Helps for the Anxious and for Young Believers

Edward Dennett

Fundamental Truths of Salvation
Being Helps for the Anxious and for Young Believers

ISBN/EAN: 9783743393844

Manufactured in Europe, USA, Canada, Australia, Japa

Cover: Foto ©Lupo / pixelio.de

Manufactured and distributed by brebook publishing software (www.brebook.com)

Edward Dennett

Fundamental Truths of Salvation

FUNDAMENTAL TRUTHS OF SALVATION:

BEING

Helps for the Anxious

AND FOR YOUNG BELIEVERS.

1876.

PREFACE.

THE following pages are designed to meet the need of those who have been awakened and quickened by the Spirit of God; and therefore the writer has sought to explain "the way of salvation" as simply and as clearly as possible. On this account he has not been anxious to avoid repetition, if in this way he could succeed in simplifying his subject. But he has not been satisfied alone with directing the soul to "the Lamb of God which taketh away the sin of the world;" but, as the table of contents will show, has added instruction upon some of the fundamental teachings of the Scriptures—*such elementary instruction as is needful for babes in Christ.* It may occur to some that other subjects might have been included. The writer also thought so; but upon further consideration was led to judge otherwise, especially as there are numbers of books already in existence which deal with more advanced truth.

FUNDAMENTAL TRUTHS OF SALVATION.

CHAPTER I.

SOUL-ANXIETY.*

WE desire in these pages to meet the need of those who have been awakened out of the torpor of spiritual death, and whose chief concern is to know how to obtain peace with God. Their state may be best described as one of soul-anxiety. There are always numbers in this condition, and especially now, when the gospel of the grace of God is so widely preached on every hand. It is not only those who are so wrought upon as to be compelled to cry, "What must we do to be saved?" but there are many others also who, under an outwardly calm and placid demeanour, hide severe distress of soul. The depth and intensity of feeling will vary in different people and under different circumstances. With some it will be anxiety, and nothing more; with others there

---

* The substance of this chapter has appeared elsewhere.

will be a real distress of mind and heart; while in other cases there will be positive anguish of soul. But whatever the depth of the feeling—be it more or less—if there be any conviction of alienation from or guilt before God; if there be any sorrow for sin, together with even but the faintest desire for pardon and reconciliation with God; if, in other words, there be any bowing before God in the place of self-judgment, there is that real spiritual anxiety of which we speak; for such a state of mind can only be produced by the Spirit of God.

The instrumentality employed to bring about this state of soul is, in one form or another, the word of God. This may not be always apparent; for sometimes a hymn, sometimes a simple question from another, sometimes the recollection of a prayer, sometimes the appeal of a preacher of the gospel, may be used as the arrow of conviction; but in all these cases it is really the word of God, embodied in these several forms, which the Holy Spirit wields to awaken the careless soul. His own word is, as far as we know, the only weapon which God uses for this end; for He is pleased "by the foolishness of preaching to save them that believe" (1 Cor. i. 21); and hence the apostle says, "We preach Christ crucified, unto the Jews a stumblingblock, and unto the Greeks foolishness; but unto them which are called, both

Jews and Greeks, Christ the power of God, and the wisdom of God." (1 Cor. i. 23, 24.)

Several illustrations of this may be collected from the Acts of the Apostles. On the day of Pentecost we find Peter presenting, in preaching, Christ crucified, risen, and exalted, and charging his hearers with the sin of rejecting and crucifying Him whom God had raised from the dead. "Therefore let all the house of Israel know assuredly, that God hath made that same Jesus, whom ye have crucified, both Lord and Christ. *Now when they heard*, they were pricked in their heart, and said unto Peter and to the rest of the apostles, Men [and] brethren, what shall we do?" (Acts ii. 36, 37.) The apostle Paul was humbled at the feet of the Saviour in a special and extraordinary way; but it was also by the presentation of Christ, though in revelation, and not in the preaching of the word. Take the case also of Felix. We are told that when the apostle reasoned of righteousness, temperance, and judgment to come, Felix trembled; and though the effect in this instance seems to have been but transient, it yet shows us the power of the word of God over the soul. The Philippian jailer might seem at first sight to be an exception to the rule; but there can be little doubt that the supernatural occurrences of that eventful night, when Paul and Silas were in his charge and custody, were but the occasion of his soul-distress—the means of fastening upon his heart and conscience the gospel message which he must have previously heard. It is often so now. Sudden sickness or danger, bringing an immediate prospect of death, will frequently give effect, under the power of the Spirit, to the previously unheeded and neglected messages and warnings of the gospel; and, filling the souls of men with guilty fears, with apprehensions of God's wrath against them, will constrain them to cry aloud for mercy.

Wherever therefore we see soul-anxiety—that soul-anxiety of which we have spoken—we may be sure that it has been wrought by the Holy Spirit through the word of God. And it is to those that are the subjects of this anxiety that we desire to speak. Beloved reader, are you in this condition of concern for salvation? Have you been convicted of sin, and is it the desire of your soul to know the way of peace with God? If such is your state, beware of turning a deaf ear to the voice of the Spirit of God, of trifling with, or seeking to hush or to drown the convictions which He has wrought. Beware also, we entreat you, of delay. God is striving in grace with you. For you, therefore, it is especially true, that "*now* is the accepted time, and *now* is the day of salvation." (2 Cor. vi. 2.) Beware, too, of healing the wounds of your soul with other remedies than those of the gospel, lest you be led to cry "Peace" when there is no peace. Your case is full of hope. For He who has awakened your desires after salvation sends this message to you, "Be ye reconciled to God" (2 Cor. v. 20); and His own word says, that "God so loved the world, that He gave His only begotten Son, that whosoever believeth in Him should not perish, but have everlasting life." (John iii. 16.) Let me then beseech you, as before God, to read, both carefully and prayerfully, the ensuing pages, that you may learn the way of salvation as revealed in the Scriptures. And may God Himself teach you, and guide you into peace, through believing in Christ!

"Rest, weary soul!
The penalty is borne, the ransom paid;
For all thy sins full satisfaction made.
Strive not thyself to do what Christ has done;
Claim the free gift, and make the joy thine own;
No more by pangs of guilt and fear distrest,
Rest, sweetly rest!"

"Jesus, we rest in Thee,
In Thee ourselves we hide;
Laden with guilt and misery,
Where could we rest beside?
'Tis on Thy meek and lowly breast
Our weary souls alone can rest."

CHAPTER II.

MAN'S STATE BEFORE GOD.

THE very first thing that anxious souls need to learn is their place and condition before God; *i.e.* to understand in what light they are regarded by God Himself. For as long as they continue deceived and ignorant of their own condition, so long will they be unwilling to be saved by God's grace. Hence, until they apprehend and receive His testimony about themselves, they will not receive His testimony about His Son. For the gospel is for *sinners*, and therefore can only be proclaimed to sinners. I would press this point very earnestly upon all who are the subjects of soul anxiety; for many are kept for months, and even years, in doubt and distress, because they search their own hearts, instead of God's word, to ascertain their real condition, and because therefore they never take the place before God which He assigns to them. "The heart is deceitful above all things" (Jer. xvii. 9); but God's word is truth (John xvii. 17); and hence it is to it alone that we must appeal.

What then is God's testimony concerning you—

concerning all men? Be prepared for the worst. It is, "By one man sin entered into the world, and death by sin; and so death passed upon all men, for that *all have sinned.*" (Rom. v. 12.) Again, "There is none righteous, no, not one: there is none that understandeth, there is none that seeketh after God. They are all gone out of the way, they are together become unprofitable; there is none that doeth good, no, not one," etc. (Rom. iii. 10-19.) Once more, "There is no difference: for *all have sinned*, and come short of the glory of God." (*vv.* 22, 23.) "The Scripture hath concluded all under sin." (Gal. iii. 22.) Such is the testimony of the Scriptures, according to which all men are sinners before God. *Do you accept it as true of yourself?*

I do not ask if you assent to it in a general way; for many will do this who will yet seek, by comparison with others, either to excuse themselves or to draw conclusions to their own advantage. The point is this, God places all men on the *same footing* before Him; He declares that all are sinners; that there is no question with Him of degrees of sinfulness or of guilt, but that there is no difference; that all, whatever their station, character, or repute, are sinners, sinners without excuse, without a single ground of hope in themselves, inasmuch as all lie under the same condemnation; for death has passed upon all men, for that all have sinned; for the wages of sin is death. (Rom. vi. 23.) Again I ask you, Do you accept this testimony of God as true of yourself? Do you bow in self-judgment before God, acknowledging that you are a sinner under His just judgment against sin?

If you do not, then I entreat you to pause and consider the hopelessness of your case; for the Lord Jesus Himself said, "I am not come to call the righteous, but sinners to repentance." (Matt. ix. 13.) There is therefore no Christ, no Saviour, except for sinners; and hence, as long as you hesitate or refuse to take the lost sinner's place, you are outside the pale of God's grace and mercy in the gospel. But if you do accept the testimony of the Scriptures as to your state, we can then tell of One who "bare our sins in His own body on the tree" (1 Peter ii. 24); "who was wounded for our transgressions, bruised for our iniquities" (Isa. liii. 5); of One "whom God hath set forth a propitiation through faith in His blood" (Rom. iii. 25); of Him, indeed, who has taken the sinner's place, borne the sinner's judgment, that whosoever believeth on Him might not perish, but have everlasting life. (2 Cor. v. 21; John iii. 16.)

But the whole truth has not yet been told. It is not only that you are sinners, but the Scriptures teach also that all who are unsaved are "dead in trespasses and sins." (Eph. ii. 1.) The Lord Jesus thus says that the believer "is passed from *death unto life*" (John v. 24), showing plainly that the previous condition of the believer was death, spiritual death. The sinner therefore is both under the condemnation of sin, and is dead in sins. It is not meant of course that he has no life at all; for it is very palpable that he has physical life. But what is asserted is, that through sin the sinner is separated from God, cut off from the source of life (for God is the Fountain of life), and consequently that the sinner is in a state of spiritual death, having no life, and no power of life towards God. The whole dealings of God with men, from Israel downwards, do but prove the truth of His word; and hence I have to ask you again, *Do you accept this further testimony concerning yourself?*

Beloved reader, you will never know the hopelessness of your condition until you subscribe also to this verdict. Men say, "While there is life there is hope." How often have such words sustained the hearts of those who have been watching by the bedside of a sick relative. Hoping against hope, they refused to believe that the end was near, and not until the last beat of the pulse, together with the last breath, would they believe that they stood in the presence of death. So also is it oftentimes with sinners; yea, even with awakened and anxious souls. They may not doubt that they are sinners, and sinners under judgment; but they cannot believe that their case is hopeless, that they have no power of life within themselves, no power of recovery, restoration, and hence they will not take the place of being utterly undone, lost, "dead in trespasses and sins." Ah! thereby they effectually shut themselves out from blessing, and turn back, it may be, to years of weary wanderings and conflicts because they believed their own hearts (and he that trusteth his own heart is a fool—Prov. xxviii. 26) rather than God. But we should resolutely close our eyes against everything but the testimony of the Scriptures; for it is not what I think, feel, or believe, but what God declares, that determines my condition in His sight. He is the sole Judge; and hence, if He tells the sinner that he is dead in trespasses and sins, it is incumbent upon the sinner to acknowledge that God is true though every man be a liar. (Rom. iii. 4.)

Do you then now believe that having no life you have no hope? If not, accept God's verdict at once; for as soon as you take the sinner's place, owning the truth of God's word about you, confessing that you are under the just judgment of sin, so soon are you in the place of blessing; the place in which God, in all His infinite grace, can meet you; the place in which you can claim the sinner's Saviour. Bow therefore before God at once, and receive the unspeakable gift of His love—His own Son, as your Saviour, Redeemer, and Lord.

"O God of mercy—Father;
  The one unchanging claim,
The brightest hopes, we gather
  From Christ's most precious name;
What always sounds so sweetly
  In Thine unwearied ear,
Has freed our souls completely
  From all our sinful fear.

"The trembling sinner feareth
  That God can ne'er forget;
But one full payment cleareth
  His memory of all debt.
When nought beside could ease us,
  Or set our souls at large,
Thy holy work, Lord Jesus,
  Secured a full discharge.

"No wrath God's heart retaineth
  To us-ward who believe;
No dread in ours remaineth
  As we His love receive.
Returning sons He kisses,
  And with His robe invests;
His perfect love dismisses
  All terror from our breasts."

CHAPTER III.

THE BLOOD OF CHRIST.

SUPPOSING now that those of whom we speak—'anxious ones'—have bowed to the judgment of God upon their condition, their immediate concern will be to know by what means they can obtain the pardon of their sins. The blood of Christ is the only way by which the guilt of sin can be removed. " *Without shedding of blood is no remission.*" (Heb. ix. 22.) Herein lies the necessity for the death of Christ; the need, in fact, for the whole work of redemption. And hence it is of the first importance that this truth should be rightly understood.

We have already pointed out that death has "passed upon all men, for that all have sinned." (Rom. v. 12.) Adam first incurred the penalty through his disobedience to God. He had been warned not to eat of the tree of the knowledge of good and evil; "for in the day that thou eatest thereof thou shalt surely die." (Gen. ii. 16, 17.) Adam disregarded the divine command, and fell under the awful sentence of death—the penalty which God had annexed to disobedience. Thus "by one man sin entered into the world, and death by sin; and so death passed upon all men, for that all have sinned." (Rom. v. 12.) There is therefore no difference; all alike are sinners; and hence every child of Adam's race is subject to the penalty of sin, which is death. Yea, death already reigns (see Rom. v. 13–21) over the whole human family: every individual member of it (saving those who believe in the Lord Jesus Christ) being under the righteous judgment of death, because of sin. "But God commendeth His love toward us, in that, while we were yet sinners, Christ died for us." (Rom. v. 8.) He "so loved the world, that He gave His only begotten Son, that whosoever believeth in Him should not perish, but have everlasting life." (John iii. 16.) Being rich in mercy, He sent His own Son to die, "the just for the unjust, that He might bring us to God." (1 Peter iii. 18.) Just as when Abraham was about to sacrifice his son, God provided a lamb to be offered up in his stead, that Isaac might be rescued and live (Gen. xxii.), so God has provided a Lamb to be offered up in the sinner's room and stead—"the Lamb of God, which taketh away the sin of the world." (John i. 29.) This is the secret and meaning, in this aspect, of the death of Christ. He died as the sinner's substitute, bore the sinner's judgment, expiated the sinner's guilt.

The marvellous efficacy of the blood of Christ,

as meeting the sinner's need, flows from the character of His person and the nature of His death. His blood is the symbol of His death, of His life poured out; for the life is in the blood (see Lev. xvii. 10–14), and hence His blood cleanses from sin, because of the value of His death before God in the sinner's place and behalf. God has condescended to teach us this by type and illustration, as well as by direct statement. Look at the Israelites in the land of Egypt on the passover night. God was about to execute judgment upon the land of Egypt; and when once He began to deal in righteousness, Israel was as much amenable to the penalty of sin as the Egyptians. How then spare the former when the latter were to be judged? "I will pass through the land of Egypt this night, and will smite all the firstborn in the land of Egypt, both man and beast; and against all the gods of Egypt I will execute judgment: I am the Lord. *And the blood shall be to you for a token upon the houses where ye are: and when I see the blood, I will pass over you*, and the plague shall not be upon you to destroy you, when I smite the land of Egypt." (Ex. xii. 12, 13; also *vv.* 21–23.) The only ground (mark it well) of difference on this night between Israel and Egypt was THE BLOOD. It was not what Israel *was* in comparison with the Egyptians, but it was the blood that stayed the destroyer's hand—the blood on the outside of their houses; for the Lord had said, When *I* see the blood, I will pass over you. The blood of the lamb—for the lamb had been slain—cleansed them typically from guilt, so that God could righteously spare Israel while He righteously destroyed Egypt. The same lesson is taught by the great day of atonement, of which we have the record in Leviticus xvi. For Aaron was directed to sprinkle the blood of the bullock, and of the goat of the sin-offerings, both upon the mercy-seat and before the mercy-seat, where God dwelt between the cherubim; "for on that day shall the priest make an atonement for you, to cleanse you, that ye may be clean from all your sins before the Lord." (Lev. xvi. 30.) All these things were but shadows of the efficacy of the blood of Christ. Thus we read: "Christ our Passover is sacrificed for us" (1 Cor. v. 7); and again, "Neither by the blood of goats and calves, but by His own blood He entered in once into the holy place, having obtained eternal redemption. For if the blood of bulls and goats, and the ashes of an heifer sprinkling the unclean, sanctifieth to the purifying of the flesh : *how much more shall the blood of Christ*, who through the eternal Spirit offered Himself without spot to God, purge your conscience from dead works to serve the living God?" (Heb. ix. 12–14.) Accordingly we are taught, that "the blood of Jesus Christ His

(God's) Son cleanseth us from all sin." (1 John i. 7.)

We may, then, now point out distinctly the teaching of Scripture as to the blood of Christ in relation to sin. (1.) It is the only means of cleansing from guilt. This is the divinely appointed and the divinely given way. *It is therefore exclusive of all other methods.* "Though thou wash thee with nitre, and take thee much sope, thine iniquity is marked before me, saith the Lord God." (Jer. ii. 22.) "If I wash myself with snow-water, and make my hands never so clean; yet shalt thou plunge me in the ditch, and mine own clothes shall abhor me." (Job ix. 30, 31.) It is only the blood of Christ which can make the sinner whiter than snow. (2.) It is the blood in and by itself alone which possesses this efficacy. There cannot be any addition to it. It is not the blood and something else. Add to it in any way, whether by feelings, prayers, penitence (all of which have their proper place), and you mar its cleansing power. (3.) God has provided the blood. It is He who has delivered up His Son to death. This provision for the sinner's need is one therefore entirely of God's grace, and consequently a provision outside of the sinner altogether. God in His infinite mercy, and because He so loved the world, provided the Lamb for the sacrifice; and now the precious blood of that Lamb avails for every one who believes. (John iii. 16.) There is no limit whatever in its application, excepting in the sinner's unbelief. It is provided for all, and everyone may be the subject of its blessed cleansing power through faith.

Beloved reader, you have confessed your need of cleansing, and God has provided that which alone can meet your need. Do you ask, But how am I to obtain the application of the blood to myself? *Solely and entirely by the obedience of faith.* Let us go back to the passover night. (Ex. xii.) It was not enough that the lamb was slain, and that the blood was in the basin; but the Israelite was directed to sprinkle the blood for himself upon the lintel and the two side-posts of his door. With the bunch of hyssop in his hand, the sign of his humiliation before the righteous judgment of God, he sprinkled the blood, thereby confessing his own desert of death, and his faith in the blood as the means to avert the stroke of the destroyer, of sheltering him from the wrath of the Righteous Judge. So now. The Lamb has been provided, and slain; His blood has been shed. But the fact of His blood-shedding does not secure your safety. The question is, *Are you under the shelter of the blood?* Do you again ask, How can this be? By bowing in humiliation, like the Israelite, before the judgment which God has pronounced against sin; that is, by taking the place of a sinner, and by looking to the blood of Christ to secure you from the righteous doom and meed of sin. The moment you do this, the blood of Christ is upon you in all its value, between you and judgment, sheltering you completely and for ever from the consequences of sin; for the blood has met and satisfied all the claims that a holy God had against you. For God hath set forth Christ a propitiation through faith in His blood. (Rom. iii. 25.) There is therefore absolutely nothing for you to do; not even have you to gather the hyssop and sprinkle the blood. You have simply to believe the word of God, to look in faith to the blood already shed, as the only means of protection from death and judgment, and God instantly sees you as covered with all its efficacy and value—cleansed from guilt, and whiter than snow. Delay not, then, to seek the protection of the precious blood of Christ. At midnight the Lord smote all the first-born in the land of Egypt; and as suddenly and unexpectedly will judgment overtake the rejecter of Christ, for when they shall say, Peace and safety, then sudden destruction cometh upon them, and they shall not escape. (1 Thess. v. 3.) To-day, then, hear the entreating voice of the love of God, which bids you to flee from the wrath to come, and to "behold the Lamb of God, which taketh away the sin of the world." (John i. 29.)

THE BLOOD OF CHRIST.

"When first o'erwhelmed with sin and shame,
  To Jesus' cross I trembling came,
  Burdened with guilt, and full of fear,
  Yet drawn by love, I ventured near,
  And pardon found, and peace with God,
  In Jesus' rich atoning blood.

"My sin is gone, my fear is o'er,
  I shun His presence now no more;
  He sits upon the throne of grace,
  He bids me boldly seek His face;
  Sprinkled upon the throne of God,
  I see that rich atoning blood.

"Before His face my Priest appears;
  My Advocate the Father hears;
  That precious blood, before His eyes,
  Both day and night for pardon cries;
  It speaks, it ever speaks to God—
  The voice of that atoning blood.

"By faith that voice I also hear;
  It answers doubt, it stills each fear:
  Th' accuser seeks in vain to move
  The wrath of Him whose name is Love;
  Each charge against the sons of God
  Is silenced by th' atoning blood.

"Here I can rest without a fear;
  By this to God I now draw near;
  By this I triumph over sin,
  For this has made and keeps me clean;
  And when I reach the throne of God,
  I'll praise that rich ATONING BLOOD."

CHAPTER IV.

YE MUST BE BORN AGAIN.

WHEN Nicodemus went to our Lord for instruction, he was met instantly by the solemn word, "Verily, verily, I say unto thee, Except a man be born again, he cannot see the kingdom of God." (John iii. 3.) It behoves therefore every anxious soul to consider this searching divine word; because we at once learn, that whatever the anxiety of soul—earnest desires, profession of faith—if there has not been wrought this great change, the "new birth," there is no life in the soul, and consequently no salvation.

Who was it then to whom the Lord addressed these words? We only learn half the truth when we answer, Nicodemus, a ruler of the Jews; for, in fact, this tells us nothing beyond his name and official rank, and these things have no weight before God, and no significance for the seeking soul. It is in the connection of the third chapter with the second that we shall find the real answer to our question. We read, "Now when He [Jesus] was in Jerusalem at the passover, in the feast-day, *many believed in His name, when they saw the miracles which He did.* But Jesus did not commit Himself unto them, because He knew all men, and needed not that any should testify of man; for He knew what was in man. *But"* (as it should be read) "there was a man of the Pharisees named Nicodemus, a ruler of the Jews," etc. (John ii. 23-25; iii. 1, etc.) There was thus a number of Jews who believed on Jesus when they saw His miracles, and Nicodemus was one of that number. But Jesus did not commit Himself to them because He knew what was in man; because, in fact, their faith was nothing more than a *natural* conviction, wrought by the evidence of the miracles, of the truth of the claims of Jesus. There was no bowing of heart before God in all this; there was nothing more than a natural or intellectual belief in the name of Christ. When therefore Nicodemus came to Jesus by night, no doubt in quest of something more, and expressed this belief, "Rabbi, we know that thou art a teacher come from God: for no man can do these miracles that thou doest, except God be with him," Jesus answered him at once by stating the necessity of being born again. It was as if He had said, "You may believe in me as a divine teacher, and yet be lost. You must be born again before you can enter into the kingdom of God."

We thus get a most solemn warning, as well as a needed caution. The warning is, "Beware of being satisfied with a profession of belief in Christ." The caution is, "Never forget that everything is useless if you have not been born again. You may be most earnest, most religious, a model of activity, in high repute for sanctity of life, or for works of usefulness, and yet be a lost soul; for unless you are born again, you cannot even see the kingdom of God."

Why then must a man be born again? The answer to this question brings us to a most important part of our subject. We have already shown that all men are sinners; but it is not only that they are sinners, but they have an evil, corrupt, depraved nature; and this incurably corrupt nature is the tree which produces all the evil fruits of sin. The acts of sin reveal the character of the nature; and this nature is totally unfit for God's presence. This is the purport of our Lord's words in this chapter, "That which is born of flesh is flesh." (*v.* 6.) All therefore that we are as natural men, as children of Adam, is flesh; and in this flesh there dwelleth no good thing. (Rom. vii. 18.)

"Are we to understand that all men, without exception, are thus totally corrupt, hopelessly evil?"

"Yes. Such is the verdict of God upon human nature. 'That which is born of flesh is flesh.'"

"But is it possible, for example, that all the noble deeds recorded in history, or all the kind, generous, and beneficent actions which we meet with in daily life, are all these done by those who have a totally depraved nature? Surely there must be a difference—degrees in our natural condition; for how is it possible to class such actions with open and flagrant sins?"

It matters not what may be the outward character of the actions of men, whether such as will elicit the applause or draw down the condemnation of their fellows; for as long as they proceed from men who have not been born again, they are nothing but evil in the sight of God, "for a corrupt tree cannot bring forth good fruit. For of thorns men do not gather figs, nor of a bramble bush gather they grapes." (Luke vi. 43, 44.) The word of God is most explicit on this question. "The carnal mind" (the mind of the flesh) "is enmity against God: for it is not subject to the law of God, neither indeed can be. *So then they that are in the flesh cannot please* God." (Romans viii. 7, 8.) It is thus, as Luther said, not a question of doing, but of *being;* not a question of the character of actions, but a question of nature, and this nature God declares to be flesh, and the flesh is nothing but evil in His sight, and consequently "flesh and blood cannot inherit the kingdom of God; neither doth corruption inherit incorruption." (1 Cor. xv. 50.)

Herein therefore lies the necessity of being born

again. "That which is born of the flesh is flesh. .... Marvel not that I said unto thee, Ye *must* be born again." (John iii. 6, 7.) This necessity is universal in its application. It concerns every one born into this world, the dutiful, obedient child as much as the prodigal son; the active, zealous philanthropist as much as the convict in his cell. For the flesh is flesh, and cannot enter the kingdom of God. There must therefore be a *new nature* and a *new life;* for if there be not these, whatever a man's moral repute, he will be for ever outside of the kingdom of God.

How then must a man be born again? This, in substance, was the question of Nicodemus. "How can a man be born when he is old? Can he enter the second time into his mother's womb, and be born?" (John iii. 4.) This question rigidly construed means undoubtedly, How is it *possible* for a man to be born again? But our Lord, in His answer, does not notice it in this form, but points out the way in which a man *is* born again. "Verily, verily, I say unto thee, Except a man be born *of water and of the Spirit*, he cannot enter into the kingdom of God." (*v.* 5.)

(1) *Water.* Much difficulty has been occasioned by special attempts to wrest the meaning of this symbol. Ritualists of many shades have persistently endeavoured to support their false teaching of baptismal regeneration from this passage. But

if we confine ourselves to the Scriptures, we shall find that the difficulty will disappear. Now it is very evident that Nicodemus should have understood what our Lord meant; and if he did not, that he was expected to understand. For when he replied, "How can these things be? Jesus answered and said, Art thou a master of Israel, and knowest not these things?" (John iii. 9, 10.) And if we turn to one of the prophets (with whose writings Nicodemus, as one of Israel's teachers, should have been well acquainted), we shall find a distinct foreshadowing of this teaching of our Lord. Speaking of the future restoration of Israel, the prophet says, "Then will I sprinkle clean water upon you, and ye shall be clean: from all your filthiness, and from all your idols, will I cleanse you. A new heart also will I give you, and a new spirit will I put within you: and I will take away the stony heart out of your flesh, and I will give you an heart of flesh. And I will put my Spirit within you, and cause you to walk in my statutes, and ye shall keep my judgments, and do them." (Ezek. xxxvi. 25–27.) Here we have the same conjunction of the water and the Spirit, and a radical change following upon its application; for nothing less than this can be implied by "a new heart." Not only so, but the water in this passage is used in the most familiar of all senses to the Israelites, in connection with cleansing.

With this passage then before us, what, we ask, is the import of the water? Turn to Psalm cxix., and we get this question: "Wherewithal shall a young man cleanse his way? by taking heed thereto *according to thy word.*" We read also in the New Testament of "the washing of water by the word" (Eph. v. 26); again, "Now ye are clean through" (or because of) "the word which I have spoken unto you." (John xv. 3; read also John xiii. 5–11.) The water therefore is a well-known symbol for the word of God. Hence we find the Word constantly associated in other passages with the new birth. "Of His own will begat He us with *the word of truth.*" (James i. 18.) "Being born again, not of corruptible seed, but of incorruptible, *by the word of God*, which liveth and abideth for ever. For all flesh is as grass, and all the glory of man as the flower of grass. The grass withereth, and the flower thereof falleth away; but the word of the Lord endureth for ever. *And this is the Word which by the gospel is preached unto you.*" (1 Peter i. 23–25.) The apostle Paul makes an allusion to the same thing when he says to the Corinthians, "In Christ Jesus I have begotten you *through the gospel.*" (1 Cor. iv. 15.) The Word of God, preached in the gospel, is the first means of the new birth which our Lord here sets forth under the type of water.

(2) *And [of] the Spirit.* "It is the Spirit that

quickeneth." (John vi. 63.) "The letter killeth, but the Spirit giveth life." (2 Cor. iii. 6.) The Spirit acting in and through the word of God quickens dead souls, and they are born again. The Word cannot do this in and by itself; nor does the Spirit of God act alone, but He wields the Word as the instrument, so that by it He may bring souls out of death into life, producing in them both a new nature and a new life. Many illustrations of this might be collected from the Scriptures. Take the most prominent of all—that afforded by the day of Pentecost. The crucifiers of the Lord Jesus were gathered round about Peter and the other apostles. Peter proclaimed the word of God to them, and said, "Let all the house of Israel know assuredly, that God hath made that same Jesus, whom ye have crucified, both Lord and Christ." (Acts ii. 36.) At the beginning of the chapter we read of the descent of the Holy Spirit; and it is said of the apostles that "they were all filled with the Holy Ghost, and began to speak with other tongues, as the Spirit gave them utterance." Peter was therefore speaking in the power of the Spirit, and that same Spirit clothed the word of God with mighty power, and the effect was that a multitude were born again, the change wrought upon them being indicated by the fact that "they were pricked in their heart, and said unto Peter and to the rest of the apostles,

Men [and] brethren, what shall we do?" (v. 37.) So it is now when men are born again. It is always through the Word, by the Spirit of God. There is no other way.

(3) We may, however, with our Lord's own teaching before us, define more exactly. In the ninth verse Nicodemus asks, "How can these things be?" Our Lord first of all rebukes, though with all tenderness, both his ignorance (v. 10) and his unbelief (vv. 11, 12), and then proceeds to vouchsafe a full reply to the question he had put. It falls into three parts, and together they reveal the whole mystery which was perplexing the mind of Nicodemus. (a) *The Person of the Son of man.* This is the foundation of all in that word of God—the gospel—by which, through the Spirit of God, souls are born again. "No man hath ascended up to heaven, but He that came down from heaven, [even] the Son of man which is in heaven." (v. 13.) We have here the great mystery of the Incarnation of the Son of God. He was in heaven, but He "came down from heaven," was born of a woman, and became the Son of man on earth, who yet while He spake to Nicodemus could say of Himself, "Who is in heaven." It is the God-man--true man, and true God, who is here revealed in the Person of the Son of man. And it is this wondrous dignity of the **Person of Christ** which gives such infinite efficacy

to His work; and hence the necessity of guarding with such jealous care the true doctrine of the Person of our Lord, of repudiating, refusing all teachings which seek to degrade either His human or divine natures. For whatever militates against the Person of Christ, militates against the cross, against His atoning sacrifice. The Person of Christ lies at the foundation of, gives its blessed character to, the gospel of the grace of God. "For God, who commanded the light to shine out of darkness, *hath shined in our hearts, to [give] the light of the knowledge of the glory of God in the face of Jesus Christ.*" (2 Cor. iv. 6.) (β) *The Work of Christ.* In this we have the second of the divine "musts." "Ye," said our Lord, "*must* be born again;" and now He says, "As Moses lifted up the serpent in the wilderness, even so MUST THE SON OF MAN BE LIFTED UP: that whosoever believeth in Him should not perish, but have everlasting life." (John iii. 14, 15.) But why must the Son of man be lifted up—crucified? It was a moral necessity; for without the shedding of blood there is no remission (Heb. ix. 22); because, as taking the sinner's place, He must be "wounded for our transgressions, bruised for our iniquities" (Isa. liii. 5); because, inasmuch as we were under the judgment and condemnation of sin, He must die in our stead; for He "bare our sins in His own body on the tree."

(1 Peter ii. 24.) It was, in a word, as the sinner's substitute that He must be "lifted up." The object of His being lifted up is, "that whosoever believeth in Him should not perish, but have eternal life." (*v.* 15.) He thus becomes the source of life, yea, in resurrection He is the life of every believer (Col. iii. 3, 4); for it is in being born again that this life is communicated through the power of the quickening Spirit. But He is the life of those who believe, because of the character of His death, because He was the sinner's substitute on the cross; for it was in death that He expiated, made atonement for our sins, and thereby removed every barrier out of the way between a God of grace and lost sinners. Hence He could say, "He that believeth in me, though he were dead, yet shall he live." (John xi. 25.) It is thus life out of death, life in a crucified and risen Saviour, because "through death He destroyed him that had the power of death" (Heb. ii. 14); for if the corn of wheat had not fallen into the ground and died, it must have remained alone; but having died, it brings forth much fruit. (John xii. 24.) (γ) *Faith* is the connecting-link between the sinner and Christ, just as the touch was the connecting-link between those who were healed and Christ in the days of His sojourn here. Hence it is, "Whosoever believeth in Him should not perish, but have eternal life." (*vv.* 15, 16.)

This will be at once understood by looking at the comparison which the Lord Himself has made. He compares His own "lifting up" to the serpent lifted up by Moses in the wilderness. (Num. xxi. 6–9.) They were serpents that bit the people of Israel and caused their death; it was a serpent to which they were directed to look and live. It is sin that has caused our death. "By one man sin entered into the world, *and death by sin,*" etc. (Rom. v. 12.) It is to One who was made sin for us (2 Cor. v. 21) on whom we are commanded to believe in order to live.

This, then, is the present point of importance—the comparison between the looking and believing. We read—"And Moses made a serpent of brass, and put it upon a pole, and it came to pass, *that if a serpent had bitten any man, when he beheld the serpent of brass, he lived.*" (Num. xxi. 9.) Notice, first of all, that it was the bitten Israelite who looked; and secondly, that he looked in the obedience of faith—believing the word of God. Just so is it with Christ lifted up. Whosoever takes the place of a sinner, acknowledging that he is "bitten," hopelessly lost by sin, if he look away in the obedience of faith to Christ, will not perish, but have eternal life. We thus, as in the case of the passover night, see that there is absolutely nothing whatever for the sinner to do; he has simply to believe the record that God has given of His Son, that God has dealt with sin in the death of Christ, and that therefore He proclaims life to every one that believeth. So soon then as the sinner has faith in the Lord Jesus Christ he is born again, he has everlasting life. (Gal. iii. 26.)

This is the method of the new birth. The gospel is preached—the word of God—which tells to a guilty race that "God so loved the world, that He gave (delivered up to death) His only begotten Son, that whosoever believeth in Him should not perish, but have everlasting life." (John iii. 16.) The Spirit clothes this message of God's grace with power. It enters the hearts of sinners; they believe, they are quickened, they are born again, they have everlasting life. (John iii. 16.)

Dear reader, Have you been born again? You surely, with this testing word before you, can have no difficulty in answering the question. If you are, your whole soul will go out in thanksgivings to God for the gift of His only begotten Son. If you are not, let me again warn you that it matters not what you are besides—you may be a good son or daughter, a loving husband or wife, a kind father or mother, and yet, not being born again, you are outside the kingdom of God, hopelessly undone and lost. Will you be satisfied in this condition? What had been the consequence if the bitten Israelites had refused to look at the serpent of brass, saying, "We may perhaps recover"? They would have died in their anguish and their sin. And so if you refuse to look to Christ, to believe in Him, there is no other remedy; and, instead of having eternal life, you will for ever perish. But if you bow to this divine necessity of being born again, acknowledging your true condition before God, and look to Christ in simple faith, you will immediately pass from death unto life.

> "Let earth and heaven agree,
>   Let men with angels join,
> To sing salvation free,
>   The work of grace divine;
> To praise the great atoning Lamb,
> And all His wondrous love proclaim.
>
> "Jesus! life-giving sound,
>   The joy of earth and heaven;
> No other help is found,
>   No other name is given,
> In which the sons of men can boast,
> But His who seeks and saves the lost.
>
> "His name the sinner hears,
>   And is from guilt set free;
> 'Tis music in his ears,
>   'Tis life and victory:
> His heart o'erflows with sacred joy,
> And songs of praise his lips employ."

CHAPTER V.

PEACE WITH GOD.

"BEING justified by faith, we have peace with God through our Lord Jesus Christ." (Rom. v. 1.) This is the conclusion at which the apostle arrives, after stating the grounds on which God is able to meet the sinner in grace, and to justify every one that believeth in Jesus. The principle involved is so important, and so necessary to be understood, that we propose to state it at length, so that anxious ones may see how carefully God has laid the foundation of peace outside of themselves altogether; that, in a word, they may perceive that the Rock on which it is grounded is Christ alone, and what He has done.

1. Justification is by faith; *i.e.* on the principle of faith in contrast with the principle of works. Much confusion of mind would be spared if this were remembered; and it is on this contrast that the apostle's whole argument is based. Thus, after depicting the state both of Gentiles and Jews, after proving that both are convicted as sinners, he says, "By the deeds of the law shall no flesh be justified in His [God's] sight." (Rom.

iii. 20.) Again, "Therefore we conclude that a man is justified by faith *without the deeds of the law*" (*v.* 28); and then, after citing the example of Abraham's justification—"Abraham believed God, and it was counted unto him for righteousness"—he tells us, "To him that *worketh not, but believeth* on Him that justifieth the ungodly, his faith is counted for righteousness." (Rom. iv. 3–5.) We have therefore the most complete contrast between the law and the gospel. The law had said, "The man that *doeth* them shall live in them" (Gal. iii. 12); but the gospel proclaims that God is the "justifier of every one that *believeth* in Jesus." (Rom. iii. 26.) It is no more therefore a question of works—of doing on man's part; for God has shown man's complete and utter failure in every position in which he has been placed. The Gentile without law, and the Jew under law, are brought in as sinners; and thus every mouth is stopped, and the whole world is become guilty before God. (Rom. iii. 19.) From this very fact, man is entirely precluded from doing anything either to recover himself, or to save himself. He is already under condemnation, lost, and hence works or doings of any kind are utterly without avail. If therefore he is now to be saved, it must be on the principle of faith; "For by grace are ye saved through faith; and that not of yourselves: it is the gift of God." (Eph. ii. 8.) He neither has, nor can he obtain by his utmost efforts, any righteousness before God; and accordingly he is shut up to God's righteousness, which is revealed in the gospel from faith to faith. (Rom. i. 17.)

It is of the first importance to apprehend this point; for it is just here that so many souls, like the Jews of old, fail. Thus, in the tenth chapter, we read that "they being ignorant of God's righteousness, and going about to establish their own righteousness, have not submitted themselves unto the righteousness of God. For Christ is the end of the law for righteousness to every one that believeth." (Romans x. 3, 4.) Until therefore souls understand that they cannot "establish their own righteousness," that "their righteousnesses are as filthy rags" before God (Isaiah lxiv. 6), they will never accept the truth, that they can only be justified on the principle of faith, that if they are saved, it must be by God in His grace towards them in Christ Jesus. But once understood, the gain is immense; for the eye will be immediately taken from self, and directed to Him who is the only Saviour: they will cease from their own doings, and be made willing to submit, on the principle of faith, to the righteousness of God.

2. We may inquire now, What is the object proposed to faith in order to justification? This is very clearly defined in Romans iv. The apostle, as we have seen, describes that Abraham believed

God, and it was counted to him for righteousness; and, furthermore, he details the circumstances and character of his faith, carefully pointing out that it was prior to circumcision, and that the law had nothing to do with the promise which he received (*vv.* 9–16); and then he says, "Now it was not written for his sake alone, that it was imputed to him; but for us also, to whom it shall be imputed, *if we believe on Him that raised up Jesus our Lord from the dead;* who was delivered for our offences, and was raised again for our justification." (*vv.* 23-25.) The object proposed to Abraham's faith was God Himself, in His promise that "he should be the heir of the world" (*v.* 13); and he, "against hope, believed in hope, that he might become the father of many nations, according to that which was spoken, So shall thy seed be. And being not weak in faith, he considered not his own body now dead, when he was about an hundred years old, neither yet the deadness of Sarah's womb: he staggered not at the promise of God through unbelief; but was strong in faith, giving glory to God; and being fully persuaded that, what He had promised, He was able also to perform. And therefore it was imputed to him for righteousness." (*vv.* 18–22.)

The object of his faith was thus a God of promise; but the object proposed to our faith is *a God of accomplishment;* for righteousness will be imputed to us "if we believe on Him that *raised up* Jesus our Lord from the dead." (*v.* 24.) God therefore is presented to the sinner in the gospel as One who has intervened in grace, provided redemption in Christ, and as testifying that Christ has been delivered for our offences, and raised again for our justification; as therefore a God of salvation, One who requires now nothing from the sinner but faith in Himself—requiring nothing because He has sent His only begotten Son, who took the whole of our responsibilities upon Himself, met in His death every claim which a holy God had against us, settled for ever the question of sin, and so glorified God that He is now able, on the foundation of that finished work of redemption, righteously to receive and justify every one that believeth. God has thus in grace, and out of the love of His own heart, provided everything for the sinner—the precious blood of Christ for his cleansing from guilt, a divine righteousness in which he can stand in His own presence—in fact, everything needed to bring the sinner out of his place of distance, guilt, and death, home unto Himself. In the gospel of His grace, He is therefore presented as a Giver, and not as a Receiver, and as the object of faith in His testimony concerning what He has wrought for us in and by His Son.

In the third chapter the blood of Christ is presented as the object of faith: "Being justified freely by His grace through the redemption that is in Christ Jesus: whom God hath set forth [to be] a propitiation *through faith in His blood.*" (Rom. iii. 24, 25.) The connection here is different. Man —all the world—has been proved to be guilty before God. (*v.* 19.) The question therefore is how to meet the claims of God as a Judge; and the answer is found in the blood of Christ, provided by the grace of God, so that the most guilty can come and be justified before Him through faith in the blood of Christ. (*vv.* 24-26.) But in the passage just considered God comes forth, as already said, as a God of salvation, satisfied with the work of Christ, He having made atonement for sin by His death, and thus presents Himself as the God of grace in redemption, and therefore as the object of the sinner's faith. And how blessedly simple it is! for what does God require from sinners? Only that they should believe in Him, that they should believe His testimony concerning what has been accomplished on their behalf by the death of His Son; at the same time offering to them, in confirmation of His testimony, the fact of the resurrection of Jesus our Lord from the dead. It is as if He said to us, "If you want a proof that Christ was delivered for your offences, that He has expiated them by His death, and that all my claims against you have been completely satisfied, behold it in His resurrection. I have raised Him from the dead, set Him down at my right hand in the glory, to convince all that He has finished the work of atonement, and that I have accepted it."

3. Every one who believes in Him is justified. "Being *justified* by faith;" *i.e.* we are by faith accounted righteous before God, righteous in Christ; for God "made Him [to be] sin for us, who knew no sin; that we might be made the righteousness of God in Him." (2 Cor. v. 21.) This is much more than cleansing from guilt, or pardon of sins, because we have in justification a positive righteousness which fits us for the presence of God. The blood of Christ, as we have seen, is the meritorious cause of this, it being on our behalf of such infinite value, having so glorified God in expiating our sins, that He righteously—in righteousness to His Son—receives, pardons, justifies, and brings us into the very place where Christ Himself is. Hence, as the apostle says elsewhere, "But of Him are ye in Christ Jesus, who of God is made unto us wisdom, and *righteousness*," etc. (1 Cor. i. 30.) For so completely are we identified with Christ before God, that His place is our place, His acceptance our acceptance; for we are in Him; and accordingly the apostle John can write, "As He is, so are we in this world." (1 John iv. 17.)

This will suffice to show the complete character

of our justification; and it may aid doubting souls to remember that it is God Himself who justifies the believer. For if He justifies us, if He is so completely satisfied with what has been done for us as to clear us from every charge, and set us down in Christ before Himself, who can condemn us? (Rom. viii. 33, 34.) Who can incriminate us? nay, who can lower by one jot or tittle the perfectness of our acceptance? God has spoken; He has declared that we are "justified by faith," and His word abideth for ever.

4. Peace is the portion of the justified. "Being justified by faith, *we have peace with God* through our Lord Jesus Christ." The words, "we have peace," do not of necessity mean that we enjoy it; for there are doubtless many justified ones before God who know but little of this peace. The meaning is that peace belongs to us, that it is made between our souls and God, that every question between Him and us is so perfectly settled, that He has nothing against us, that peace therefore is our portion.

But if it is made, and it belongs to us, what hinders so many souls from entering into its possession? Simply unbelief; they look within to their own state, instead of without to what God has done for them. We can only enjoy this peace as knowing it to be ours; and we can only know it to be ours by believing God's word. But if we believe, and are justified, we have peace, whatever our feelings or experience; and hence we should rest in the enjoyment of it in simple confidence in the word of God. It is of the first importance to know that it is ours; for souls are tossed hither and thither by doubts and fears, because they hesitate to believe in the fulness of the grace of God. They are therefore weak and helpless, the easy prey of the tempter; whereas if they but quietly rested on this sure word of God that they "*have* peace," that He has made it through the work of Christ, and made it for them, they would be able to sing amid the storm, to present a fearless front in the face of all difficulties, to be undisturbed by the most insidious suggestions of Satan, knowing that as the peace rests upon the cross of Christ, it is both sure and steadfast, inalienable and immutable, a foundation on which they might "build and rest secure" for ever. For the peace of the justified is the result of *accomplished* redemption, founded on the cross, and proved by the resurrection of Christ.

It may encourage some to a stronger confidence if we remind them that God is *just*, as well as the justifier of every one that believes in Jesus (Rom. iii. 26); *i.e.* that He is just to the claims which the work of Christ, or rather Christ in His work, has established upon Him. It is therefore what Christ has gained for us; and hence He is our peace. (Eph. ii. 14.) It should indeed be never forgotten that this peace is not apart from, but in and through Christ; or, consequently, that it is a righteous peace, a peace which God righteously bestows upon and secures to us through our Lord Jesus Christ.

"Blessèd be God, our God!
Who gave for us His well-beloved Son,
The gift of gifts, all other gifts in one.
Blessèd be God, our God!

"He sparèd not His Son!
'Tis this that silences each rising fear,
'Tis this that bids the hard thought disappear—
He sparèd not His Son!

"Who shall condemn us now?
Since Christ has died, and risen, and gone above,
For us to plead at the right hand of Love,
Who shall condemn us now?

"'Tis God that justifies!
Who shall recall the pardon or the grace,
Or who the broken chain of guilt replace?
'Tis God that justifies!

"The victory is ours!
For us in might came forth the Mighty One,
For us He fought the fight, the triumph won:
The victory is ours!"

CHAPTER VI.

"WHAT MUST I DO TO BE SAVED?"

HAVING pointed out God's provision for the need of souls, we may now consider the subject from man's point of view. No sooner indeed is he convicted of sin than the question springs up within his heart in one form or another, "What must I do?" It was so on the day of Pentecost, when the Jews were pricked in their heart by the power of the Holy Spirit under the preaching of Peter. "Men and brethren," they said, "what shall we do?" The jailor asked Paul and Silas, "What must I do to be saved?" (Acts xvi. 30.) Twice our Lord Himself was asked, "What shall I do that I may inherit eternal life?" (Mark x. 17; and Luke x. 25.) The question addressed to our Lord by Paul, or rather Saul—"Lord, what wilt thou have me to do?" (Acts. ix. 6)—is different, and need not therefore be considered.

The peculiarity of these questions is that the "I" occupies a prominent place, or rather perhaps the thought of doing. It is, What must I *do?* a sure sign that the questioners have not yet learnt what God is, or their true place before Him.

It is on this very account the more important to answer the question, because it marks in many souls a distinct stage of their history. There are very few indeed who have not asked the same question at some period of their soul-anxiety. We propose therefore to examine some of the examples which we have cited, that we may ascertain the answer given to it in the word of God.

1. We take first the case of the young man. (Mark x. 17; Matt. xix. 16; Luke xviii. 18.) We read that when Jesus "was gone forth into the way, there came one running, and kneeled to Him, and asked Him, Good Master, what shall I do that I may inherit eternal life? And Jesus said unto him, Why callest thou me good? [there is] none good but one, [that is,] God. Thou knowest the commandments, Do not commit adultery, Do not kill, Do not steal, Do not bear false witness, Defraud not, Honour thy father and mother. And he answered and said unto Him, Master, all these things have I observed from my youth." (Matthew tells us that the young man added, "What lack I yet?") "Then Jesus beholding him loved him, and said unto him, One thing thou lackest: go thy way, sell whatsoever thou hast, and give to the poor, and thou shalt have treasure in heaven: and come, take up the cross, and follow me. *And he was sad at that saying, and went away grieved:*

for he had great possessions." (Mark x. 17-22.) This case is the more remarkable and instructive from the fact that this young man was so blameless and unexceptionable in conduct and character. He was both sincere and upright, one who could say, what Paul said of himself, that touching the righteousness which was in the law, he was blameless (Phil. iii. 6); for he replied to our Lord's enumeration of the commandments, " All these have I observed from my youth," and added, " What lack I yet ?" (See Matt. xix. 20.)

Is not this a picture of many in our own day, young people and others, whose whole lives, morally, as we speak, in their outward expression leave nothing to be desired ? Gentle, amiable, and loving; observant, and tenderly observant of their duties as sons or daughters, upright and honourable in all the relationships of life, and diligent also in attendance upon what are termed religious duties, they win the approbation of their whole circle, both of relatives and friends. And what lack they yet ? The Lord's answer to this young man is the answer to our question. What then is its import ? First, *that man can bring nothing to God*, and therefore can DO NOTHING to inherit eternal life. Like Paul, he must learn that his righteousness is as filthy rags, to count the things which were a gain to him as a natural man loss for Christ, that nothing that he is, or has done, is of any merit before God; nay, that his best things must be regarded as worthless and unclean. Secondly, *that he must be willing to suffer the loss of all things—self, his own righteousness, and the world —for the excellency of the knowledge of Christ Jesus.* Hence our Lord told the young man to sell all that he had, and give to the poor; and then to "come, take up the cross, and follow me."

Such is the first answer to the question, "What must I do to inherit eternal life?" You must take the place of having nothing, and being nothing—self, the world, yea, and every thing being nothing—at the feet of Jesus. And let not the solemn warning of this whole incident be forgotten, that moral attainments, and the advantages of position, etc., are to be classed among the greatest hindrances to coming to Christ, because they so often cover up and conceal the soul's real condition before God.

2. The case of the lawyer. (Luke x.) This is in many respects totally different from that just considered; for the lawyer comes tempting Christ, and thus occupying a much lower moral place. Accordingly our Lord connects with it much deeper lessons of man's true condition. "A certain lawyer stood up, and tempted him, saying, Master, what shall I do to inherit eternal life? He said unto him, What is written in the law? How readest thou? And he answering said, Thou

shalt love the Lord thy God with all thy heart, and with all thy soul, and with all thy strength, and with all thy mind; and thy neighbour as thyself. And He said unto him, Thou hast answered right: this do, and thou shalt live. But he, willing to justify himself, said unto Jesus, And who is my neighbour?" etc. Then follows the parable of the "good Samaritan." (Luke x. 25-37.) Here the Lord takes the lawyer, who was tempting Him, on his own ground; viz that of the law; and He thus accepts his statement of the requirements of the law, adding the words connected with its promulgation, "This do, and thou shalt live" ("which if a man do, he shall live in them." Lev. xviii 5). But he used the law, according to its divine intention, as a standard of God's requirements from men in the flesh, and so brought in the knowledge of sin. (Rom. iii. 20.) For His words, "Thou hast answered right: this do, and thou shalt live" (*v.* 28), convicted the tempting lawyer of sin; for we read, "He, willing to *justify* himself, said unto Jesus, And who is my neighbour?" The Lord had searched him with that word which "is quick, and powerful, and sharper than any two-edged sword, piercing even to the dividing asunder of soul and spirit, and of the joints and marrow, and is a discerner of the thoughts and intents of the heart" (Heb. iv. 12);

but instead of bowing to it he desired to escape from its application, if not to insinuate the impossible character of the divine requirements. He sought to justify himself, as if a man could be just with God, by alleging that, since he could not carry out the divine command, he could not be expected to do any thing. But the Lord had brought into his mind the knowledge of sin, and then, to teach also the lesson as to who was his neighbour, described the man who fell among thieves, and how he was succoured by a Samaritan.

What then are the special lessons taught by this answer to the question, What must I do to inherit eternal life? It is not only that man can do nothing, *but that he is also convicted as a sinner before God;* and hence we have man's condition as a sinner pictured out in the parable. It is thus described: "A certain man went down from Jerusalem to Jericho, and fell among thieves, which stripped him of his raiment, and wounded [him], and departed, leaving [him] half dead." (*v.* 30.) The very place in which the traveller is assailed is significant. He was on his way from Jerusalem, the city of God, to Jericho, the city of curse (Joshua vi. 26)—a striking picture of the sinner's journey to destruction. He falls among thieves, who strip, wound, and depart, leaving him half dead; and so he lies helpless and hopeless, at the point of death.

Who does not see in this sketch man's condition as a sinner? And what folly it were for one in that condition to ask, What shall *I do* to inherit eternal life? The question rather is, What can *be done* to save him? And this is what our Lord would teach the lawyer—the folly of a sinner asking what he can do, and that if he is saved, it must be by the grace and by the doing of another. This latter truth is brought out in the Samaritan. But first a priest and a Levite pass by, and leave the wretched man to his fate, showing the helplessness of law to save the soul. Then the Samaritan comes upon the scene, "And when he saw him, he had compassion [on him], and went to [him], and bound up his wounds, pouring in oil and wine, and set him on his own beast, and brought him to an inn, and took care of him. And on the morrow when he departed, he took out two pence, and gave them to the host, and said unto him, Take care of him; and whatsoever thou spendest more, when I come again, I will repay thee." (*vv.* 33–35.) Who then is the Samaritan? Surely none but Christ—Christ, in the compassion of His love, seeking and saving the lost. For He is moved with pity by the wretchedness of the poor, helpless man, binds up his wounds, carries him to a place of safety, cares, undertakes, and provides for him until He returns. We learn therefore from the whole scene (1) that man is a sinner; (2) that as a sinner he is both helpless and lost; (3) that therefore he can do nothing; and (4) that if he is to be saved, it can only be through Christ, and what He has done.

3. This will prepare us for the case of the jailor. (Acts xvi.) We take this rather than that of the Jews on the day of Pentecost, because the question is put by him in its most distinct form. Paul and Silas, at the instigation of an excited crowd, had been put into prison at Philippi; and at midnight, we read, the apostles prayed, and sang praises to God: and "suddenly there was a great earthquake, so that the foundations of the prison were shaken: and immediately all the doors were opened, and every one's bands were loosed." (Acts xvi. 25–26.) The keeper of the prison was terrified, and in the excitement of the moment, thinking that the prisoners had escaped, would have killed himself, but for the interposition of Paul. "Then he called for a light, and sprang in, and came trembling, and fell down before Paul and Silas, and brought them out, and said, *Sirs, what must I do to be saved?* And they said, Believe on the Lord Jesus Christ, and thou shalt be saved, and thy house." (*vv.* 27–31.)

Why do Paul and Silas treat him otherwise than our Lord dealt with the two cases already considered? The answer in each case meets the moral condition of the questioner. But Paul and

Silas *are able to direct the jailor instantly to Christ, because he came in the moral condition set forth by the dying man in the parable.* And hence if any of my readers are putting this same question, they cannot be answered until they take the same place. This truth has already been insisted on in the second chapter; but we again emphasize it here. For until the lesson is learnt the way of salvation cannot be known. Are you then, beloved readers, recognizing, not only that you can bring nothing to God, that even the things that might be a gain to you amongst men are worthless before Him, but also that you are sinners, and as such lost and undone; that therefore you can do nothing towards your salvation, and that if you are saved, it must be by the work and grace of another? If you are, we can then unfold to you the blessed truth, contained in the words, "Believe on the Lord Jesus Christ, and thou shalt be saved." (*v.* 31.)

To be saved therefore, to have eternal life, you must believe on the Lord Jesus Christ. It is thus a question not of *doing*, but of *believing*. For it is now, not what the sinner can do, but what Christ has done, for "He took what I had earned; I get the fruit of what He has done." Therefore it is, and ever must be, "Believe on the Lord Jesus Christ, and thou shalt be saved." There is no other way; and hence salvation is always connected with faith. Take a few instances: "Thy faith hath saved thee; go in peace" (Luke vii. 50); "Arise, go thy way: thy faith hath made thee whole" (Luke xvii. 19); "He that believeth on the Son hath everlasting life" (John iii. 36); "He that heareth my word, and believeth on Him that sent me, hath everlasting life, and shall not come into condemnation (judgment); but is passed from death unto life" (John v. 24); "Verily, verily, I say unto you, He that believeth on me hath everlasting life" (John vi. 47); "To Him give all the prophets witness, that through His name whosoever believeth in Him shall receive remission of sins" (Acts x. 43); "Being justified by faith, we have peace with God through our Lord Jesus Christ." (Rom. v. 1, etc. etc.)

Do you then, beloved reader, believe on the Lord Jesus Christ? We have pointed out the place the sinner must first take; that he must accept God's testimony concerning himself—that he is both helpless, guilty, and lost. If you accept God's word as to yourself and your condition, we then point you to the Lamb of God which taketh away the sin of the world; for He who declares to us what we are by nature and practice in His sight, has provided redemption for us in Christ: He "so loved the world, that He gave His only begotten Son, that whosoever believeth in Him should not perish, but have everlasting life." (John iii. 16.)

Look away therefore from yourself to Christ, accept God's testimony also concerning Him, and even while you look you shall pass from death unto life. "The word is nigh thee, in thy mouth, and in thy heart: that is, the word of faith, which we preach; that if thou shalt confess with thy mouth the Lord Jesus, and shalt believe in thine heart that God hath raised Him from the dead, thou shalt be saved. For with the heart man believeth unto righteousness; and with the mouth confession is made unto salvation." (Rom. x. 8–10.)

> "'Tis finishèd! the creature owed
>   A debt he ne'er could pay to God;
>   Our sins had moved the wrath of heaven:
>   That debt is paid, those sins forgiven.
> The Son of God hath suffer'd in our stead,
>   And we are free; 'tis finishèd.
>
> "'Tis finishèd! the mighty Son
>   O'er death and hell the victory won:
>   He died, He lives for our salvation,
>   And we may say with exultation,—
> 'For me my Saviour's precious blood was shed,
>   And come what will, 'tis finishèd.'"

CHAPTER VII.

DIFFICULTIES.*

No sooner is the soul awakened, convinced of sin, and directed to Christ, than difficulties will often appear on every side, threatening deprivation for ever of the blessing now so earnestly desired. Magnified by the unbelief which is native to our hearts, and pressed continually upon the soul by the activity of Satan, they seem insuperable; and it may therefore be helpful, if the most prevalent forms which they assume are indicated and explained. At the same time it should never be forgotten that the only effectual solver of difficulties is the Lord Himself; and that they will soon cease to harass the mind, if carried and spread out in simple faith before the throne of grace.

1. "*My sins have been too many and too grievous.*" How often are words like these uttered by the self-judged penitent when he is told of the freeness of God's grace in Christ Jesus. "Yes," he will say, "Christ is able to save, and God no doubt waits to be gracious. But I am very guilty. I have sinned against light and knowledge; others may come

---

* A small portion of this chapter has appeared elsewhere.

and be saved; but for me there is no hope." Two or three remarks will show the real nature of this feeling. In the first place, it really expresses a doubt concerning the efficacy of the precious blood of Christ; for if it cannot cleanse you, it cannot cleanse from *all* sin. Moreover, it distrusts the sincerity of God in the invitations which He sends to sinners through the gospel of His grace. For He says, "Whosoever believeth in Christ shall not perish, but have everlasting life" (John iii. 16); "Whosoever will, let him take the water of life freely" (Rev. xxii. 17); and if you say that you are not included in these "whosoevers," what is it but to doubt the truth of God? Again, our Lord Himself says, "I am not come to call the righteous, but sinners to repentance." (Matt. ix. 13.) This is not some, but ALL sinners. Hence, to be a sinner, is to have a title to come to Christ; and thus the more sure you are of your sinfulness, the more certain you ought to be that there is nothing in your case to shut you out from the mercy of God.

It is worthy of question whether the root of such a feeling is not self-righteousness, for it really means that you are too unworthy. As another has said, "If when God speaks I refuse to believe on the ground of something in myself, I make Him a liar. (1 John v. 10.) When God declares His love, and I refuse to believe because I do not deem myself a sufficiently worthy object, I . . . .

exhibit the inherent pride of my heart. . . . God's love flows forth spontaneously. It is not drawn forth by my deserts, but by my misery. Nor is it a question as to the place which I deserve, but which Christ deserves. Christ took the sinner's place on the cross, that the sinner might take His place in the glory. Christ got what the sinner deserved, that the sinner might get what Christ deserves. Thus *self* is totally set aside."

Besides, it may be added, our Lord has met by anticipation your objection, by receiving while on earth some of the vilest and most degraded. The woman who was "a sinner" (Luke vii. 37–39), and the thief on the cross (Luke xxiii. 40–43) are everlasting monuments of His willingness to receive the guiltiest. Meet therefore all such thoughts by the plain examples and statements of God's word; and never harbour, even for a moment, any suggestion which tends to obscure the Saviour's willingness to receive, or His ability to save, any and all who come in penitence to His feet.

2. "*I do not feel my sins enough.*" This is quite true; for it is a complaint that even believers have to make, and will make to the end of their days upon earth. It is sure therefore to be the case with every anxious one; and it is on account of his sinfulness that he does not feel more deeply. But this only argues his greater

and more urgent need of Christ. For his want of feeling is but the evidence of his alienation from God, and consequently of his need of reconciliation through the blood of Christ. It cannot then be, that to feel deeply is a qualification for coming to Christ, for that would mean that we must first cleanse ourselves from some part of our sinfulness. No; the gospel makes no conditions with men about feelings; it demands no preparation of heart, but proclaims a present salvation to every one that believeth.

"But must I not first repent?" Let me then ask, What is meant by repentance? It is simply taking the place of self-judgment, the place of a sinner before God, taking God's view about my sins. The confusion arises from the misconception that it signifies "the feeling sorry for, and the determination to forsake, sin;" and hence many probe themselves to discover whether they are in this state of mind. But the only thing you have to consider is, Do I know that I am a sinner? and, Do I accept God's judgment of myself as a sinner? If you do, there is nothing on God's part between you and the sinner's Saviour. For the only message of the gospel is, Believe on the Lord Jesus Christ, and thou shalt be saved, and thy house. (Acts xvi. 31.)

3. "*I cannot be sure that Christ died for me; that I am personally included in the invitations of*

DIFFICULTIES.

the gospel." And why not? For when God speaks in His word so repeatedly, and says, "WHOSOEVER believeth" shall be saved (John iii. 15, 16, 36; Acts x. 43, etc.), is it not as evident that you are included as if your name were written there? As an evangelist recently put it, if you saw written over a gate, *Whosoever will may enter*, you would understand at once that you had a title to entrance; and you would regard it as downright folly if a companion were to argue with you on the subject, contending that the notice was not distinct. When then we read in the Scriptures, "Whosoever will, let him take the water of life freely" (Rev. xxii. 17), it is nothing but rank unbelief to express the doubt whether we are included in the invitation. In a recently published memoir there is an example of the kind. The subject of it, when first awakened, had this difficulty; and, though Scripture after Scripture was pressed upon him, remained immovable. But going home, he spent a great part of the night alone with God. At last he took a piece of paper, and wrote, "As I live, saith the Lord God, I have no pleasure in the death of the wicked" (Ezekiel xxxiii. 11); then he added, "I am one of the wicked;" and further, "Therefore the Lord God has no pleasure in my death," and was thus led to believe that he was within the range of the divine mercy.

Every sinner is entitled to adopt the same plan.

E

Let any one therefore who is troubled with the doubt named take, for example, John iii. 16, and write it out with self-application, and he will find that it is as clear as noonday that God includes him in the term "whosoever." There is no limit indeed to God's grace in the gospel, except in the unbelief of sinful hearts.

4. "*It may be that I am not one of the elect.*" Now this is the most useless of all doubts, except indeed for the purposes of Satan. For secret things belong unto God, and no amount of speculation or reasoning can discover them. And let it be remembered that the sinner has nothing whatever to do with God's purposes. Election has to do with saints, and saints alone. The difficulty, if sincerely felt, should therefore be met by the simple question, Am I a sinner? For if that can be plainly answered, it has already been abundantly shown that the invitations of the gospel are addressed to *you*, and that to be a sinner is the only qualification for coming to Christ.

5. "*I cannot believe.*" Let us examine this difficulty. What then is it that you cannot believe? Cannot you believe that you are a sinner? God testifies this to you in His word; and if you want any confirmation of His truth, the experience of a single day will surely be sufficient. No; you do not doubt that you are a

sinner. Can you not then believe God's testimony concerning His Son? What is that testimony? It is that "He was delivered for our offences, and was raised again for our justification (Rom. iv. 25); that "He hath once suffered for sins, the just for the unjust, that He might bring us to God" (1 Peter iii. 18); that God "made Him [to be] sin for us, who knew no sin, that we might be made the righteousness of God in Him." Do you believe this? You will say, "Of course I do." Then see what this involves. You believe on the one hand that you are a sinner, and on the other that Christ has died for sinners; and yet you say "you cannot believe." Let me then put another question. Do you believe that God is satisfied with and has accepted that which Christ has done for sinners by His death? Before you attempt to answer this question, remember two things; first, that the resurrection of Christ, and His glorification at the right hand of the Majesty on high, is the proof that God is satisfied—that He has abundantly accepted the atonement made on the cross; and secondly, that the proclamation of the gospel is a proof also of it, for the gospel is a consequence of the finished work of Christ, and its acceptance by God. It is on the foundation of the cross that the message is sent forth, "Be ye reconciled to God." (2 Cor. v. 20.) Do you then believe that God is satisfied? You cannot doubt it. What remains? *That you also should be satisfied.* This and nothing more.

"Cannot believe," therefore, often means unwillingness to believe, the refusal to bow before God's judgment upon yourself as a sinner; for when you have truly taken the place of a sinner, you must of necessity welcome the offers of salvation as glad tidings of great joy. Suppose now a family in a state of starvation at the point of death, and provision is carried to their doors, and freely offered to them, what would you think if they were to reply, "We cannot believe it is for us"? Of a like character is the objection of the sinner under condemnation to the invitations of the gospel, "I cannot believe." For remember it is God who speaks, and is it possible for unbelief to go so far as to doubt whether He is worthy of credit? If a friend were to come to you with some announcement, and you were to reply, "I cannot believe you," he would regard it, if spoken in seriousness, as an insult. Much more, then, should you hesitate to doubt the truth and veracity of God.

6. "*I cannot feel that I am saved.*" This is often said by those who think and avow that they believe in Christ, but who yet have no peace. How then is the knowledge of salvation to be obtained? Many expect some sudden accession of joy, or some inward experience to certify them of

it. A young believer once came to the writer, and said, "I know I am saved now, because I feel so happy." But when he replied, "Suppose you feel unhappy to-morrow, will you come and say, 'I know I am not saved now, because I feel so miserable'?" she at once saw that she was building on a wrong foundation. How then can it be known? *By faith*—faith in the word of God. For when God testifies that "whosoever believeth in Christ should not perish, but have everlasting life" (John iii. 16), I am entitled, if I believe, to say that I am saved, resting my confidence on this word; and peace comes as the result of my belief of God's testimony.

Such is the divine order. First, faith in the Lord Jesus Christ; secondly, knowledge of salvation, or assurance, as it is sometimes termed, from belief in the word of God; and lastly, peace as the consequence of knowing that I am saved. Take a simple illustration. If I owe a debt of one hundred pounds, and have not wherewith to meet it, I shall be under constant concern and anxiety. If however a friend comes and says, "Be under no concern for the debt. I have discharged it," my anxiety will instantly cease, *if I believe his word*, not otherwise. So is it with our knowledge of salvation. If I believe in Christ Jesus, I shall know that all God's claims against me have been satisfied, and consequently I shall.

have peace, if I believe His word, and in no other way. It is most important to apprehend this point; for many, making "assurance" to depend on feeling, are continually in a state of disquiet and unrest. But when we see that the foundation of our confidence lies in the immutable truth of God, we shall never doubt our salvation, whatever the chequered character of our inward experiences. The fact indeed is too often lost sight of (as pointed out in another chapter), that the ground of our peace is entirely outside of ourselves, in the work of Christ *for* us; and hence the eye is turned inward, instead of outward to His cross, His precious blood. "Being justified by faith, we have peace with God through our Lord Jesus Christ." (Rom. v. 1.)

It will be observed that we have spoken only of the ground of assurance. Having peace, there will be, indeed should be, happy experiences; for God sends His Spirit to dwell in the hearts of saved ones, and He bears witness with their spirits that they are the children of God. But happy experiences must follow upon, and cannot precede, the knowledge that we are saved.

7. "*Blasphemy against the Holy Ghost.*" As very many anxious souls are perplexed with the fear that they have been guilty of this sin, and that they are consequently shut out from the offers of mercy in the gospel, it may be well to explain

its true character. The words in which our Lord describes it are these: "All manner of sin and blasphemy shall be forgiven unto men: but the blasphemy against the Holy Ghost shall not be forgiven unto men. And whosoever speaketh a word against the Son of man, it shall be forgiven him: but whosoever speaketh against the Holy Ghost, it shall not be forgiven him, neither in this world, neither in the world to come." (Matt. xii. 31, 32; see also Mark iii. 28-30.)

The sin then spoken of is "blasphemy," or "speaking against" the Holy Ghost, and the precise force of these terms may be gathered from an examination of the context. The Saviour had just performed a miracle. We read, "Then was brought unto Him one possessed with a devil, blind, and dumb: and He healed him, insomuch that the blind and dumb both spake and saw." (Matt. xii. 22.) The people were deeply impressed with this display of divine power and mercy, and saw in it an evidence of His Messiahship; for they said, "Is not this the Son of David?" But the enemies of Christ—the Pharisees—made it an occasion for the exhibition of their enmity, and with the miracle before their eyes—indeed, confessing it—ascribed the power which they had seen exerted to the devil. They said, "This fellow doth not cast out devils, but by Beelzebub the prince of the devils." Hence it is that we find in the gospel of

Mark the reason given for the Saviour's warning concerning "blasphemy against the Holy Ghost:" "Because they said, He hath an unclean spirit." The sin therefore spoken of is *the wilful ascription to Satan of the power wrought by the Holy Ghost, and therefore blaspheming the Holy Ghost by maligning His operations as devilish.* To prevent all possibility of mistake, the argument may be displayed at length.

1. The power in which Jesus laboured, wrought miracles, performed His mission, was that of the Holy Spirit. (Luke iv. 1-18; Isaiah lxi. 1, 2; John iii. 34; xiv. 10, &c.)

2. It was, therefore, by the power of the Spirit of God that He expelled the devil from the blind and dumb man.

3. The Pharisees acknowledged the miracle; they had seen it done, and could not deny it.

4. They had therefore before them a clear proof of the Saviour's mission; for, if done, it substantiated His claim to be the Messiah.

5. They ignored the evidence, and sought to discredit Jesus by charging Him with being the agent of the devil.

6. They thus wilfully not only sinned against, but "blasphemed," the Holy Ghost.

Thus, as another has said, "What the Lord denounces is *blasphemy* against the Holy Ghost. Keeping that distinctly in view would save many souls a great deal of needless trouble. How many have groaned in terror through fear of being guilty of sin against the Holy Ghost! That phrase admits of vague notions and general reasonings about its nature. But our Lord spoke definitely of blasphemous, unforgivable sin against Him. All sin, I presume, is sin against the Holy Ghost, who has taken His place in Christendom, and consequently gives all sin this character. Thus, lying in the church is not mere falsehood toward man, but unto God, because of the great truth that the Holy Ghost is there. Here, on the contrary, the Lord speaks of unforgivable sin (not that vague sense of evil which troubled souls dread as "sin against the Holy Ghost," but blasphemy against Him). What, is this evil never to be forgiven? It is attributing the power that wrought in Jesus to the devil. How many troubled souls would be instantly relieved if they laid hold of that simple truth! It would dissipate what really is a delusion of the devil, who strives hard to plunge them into anxiety, and drive them into despair, if possible. The truth is, that as any sin of a Christian may be said to be sin against the Holy Ghost, what is especially *the* sin against the Holy Ghost, if there be anything which is so, is that which directly hinders the free action of the Holy Ghost in the work of God, or in His church. Such might be said to be *the* sin, if you speak of it with precision. But what our Lord referred to was neither a sin nor *the* sin, but *blasphemy against the Holy Ghost*. It was that which the Jewish nation was then rapidly falling into, and for which they were neither forgiven then, nor will ever be forgiven. There will be a new stock, so to speak; another generation will be raised up, who will receive the Christ whom their fathers blasphemed; but as far as that generation was concerned, they were guilty of this sin, and could not be forgiven. They began it in the lifetime of Jesus; they consummated it when the Holy Ghost was sent down and despised. They still carried it on persistently; and it is always the case when men enter upon a bad course, unless sovereign grace deliver. The more God brings out of love, grace, truth, wisdom, the more determinedly and blindly they rush on to their own perdition. So it was with Israel. So it ever is with man left to himself, and despising the grace of God. "He that shall blaspheme against the Holy Ghost hath never forgiveness." It is the final stage of rebellion against God."

It may then be confidently affirmed, that no one under convictions of sin, no one who desires reconciliation to God through the blood of Christ, can have committed "blasphemy against the Holy Ghost." Nay, these very convictions of sin, and desires after peace with God, are the effects of His own work in the soul; the sure proof that this "blasphemy" has not been committed.

The "sin unto death." This is popularly confounded with that just considered. But an examination of the Scripture in which it is mentioned will show that it is a totally distinct thing. It is thus described: "If any man see his brother sin a sin [which is] not unto death, he shall ask, and He shall give him life for them that sin not unto death. *There is a sin unto death:* I do not say that he shall pray for it." (1 John v. 16.) Here the question is concerning the sin of a believer. If any man see *his brother*, etc.; and since it is a believer who is spoken of, there can be no reference to eternal death. In fact, the death spoken of is bodily. Thus Ananias and Sapphira committed a sin "unto death." (Acts v.) Their sin was of such a character that God interposed and removed them from off the scene, in merciful chastisement upon themselves, and in solemn warning to others. But though they sinned "unto death," this did not affect their standing, if they were real believers. Their death was the result of the interposition of God in governmental discipline in the church on earth. Allusion is made to other cases of a similar character in 1 Corinthians. The apostle, writing concerning the abuses of the Lord's Supper, says, " He that eateth and drinketh unworthily, eateth and drinketh damnation" (*judgment,* as in margin) " to himself, not discerning the Lord's body. For this cause many are weak and sickly among you, and *many sleep.*" (1 Cor. xi. 29, 30.) That is, as the result of God's intervention in discipline, many had died.

It will be seen from the above explanation that no one can tell beforehand what constitutes the "sin unto death," because it is judged only by the Lord. Indeed, it does not follow that the same act would constitute the same sin in different circumstances; for there is little doubt that there have been many Ananiases and Sapphiras since their day. But we need not pursue the subject, as we have shown that the sin is that of a believer, and that it is connected with bodily, and not eternal, death, and hence that anxious ones cannot have been guilty of it before God.

8. *The case supposed in Heb.* vi. 3–6 is often a real difficulty. But a careful examination of the passage, though we cannot here go into it minutely, will show that it can have no application to those who are anxious and who desire peace with God. For the case is that of "those who were once enlightened, and have tasted of the heavenly gift, and were made partakers of the Holy Ghost, and have tasted the good word of God, and the powers of the world to come, if they shall fall away, to renew them again unto repentance; seeing they crucify to themselves the Son of God afresh, and put Him to an open shame." Let it be first of all distinctly noted, *that this cannot refer to the falling*

away of any who have been really converted. For nothing is more plainly taught in the Scriptures than that it is impossible for a child of God to perish. (See John x. 27-29; Rom. viii. 28-39; 1 Cor. i. 8, 9; Eph. i. 13, 14; Phil. i. 6, 7, etc., etc.) It must be borne in mind indeed that the epistle was addressed to Hebrew Christians; and the case put is that of those who had been brought out of Judaism, and convinced of the truth of Christianity, thus far enlightened by the power of the Holy Ghost, but not converted, born again. They were brought into the blessings indicated, but were still without life; and it is concerning these we are told, that if they should fall away it would be impossible to renew them again unto repentance, etc. And why? Because they would be deliberately and wilfully going back to what they knew to be no longer according to God; reassociating themselves with the nation that crucified the Son of God, and thus, by endorsing with their eyes open the act of the nation, crucifying *for themselves* the Son of God, and putting Him to an open shame. (*v.* 6.)

The case supposed therefore is that of wilful apostates. But no doubt it is intended as a solemn warning, though not for anxious souls. The warning will have its application to many who are associated with believers in various ways, to professors, and such professors as have been the subjects of much enlightenment without being born again, so that they, knowing the divine character of redemption, are persuaded that the only way of salvation is through a crucified and risen Saviour, and may even be outwardly zealous for Christ. It is for such that this warning is intended; for if they turn their backs upon what they know to be true, deny Him whom they know to be the Christ of God, *become wilful apostates*, their case is hopeless. It is to this class alone that this passage applies; and it therefore cannot include those who, convicted of sin by the Spirit of God, desire above all things to know that Christ is their Saviour and Lord. In a word, no one who desires to be saved, through faith in the Lord Jesus Christ, can be of that class and character.

There are doubtless many other difficulties in special cases, but those dealt with are the most common. Our aim should be to bring everything to the word of God in a prayerful spirit; for "unto the upright there ariseth light in the darkness" (Ps. cxii. 4), and "the entrance of thy words giveth light." (Ps. cxix. 130.)

> "Thine arm hath safely brought us
>   A way no more expected,
> Than when thy sheep pass'd thro' the deep,
>   By crystal walls protected.
> We sing thine arm unshorten'd,
>   Brought thro' each sore temptation;
> With heart and voice in thee rejoice,
>   Thou God of our salvation."

CHAPTER VIII.

DELIVERANCE.

MANY who have been awakened, quickened, and who may even be under the sure protection of the blood of Christ, are yet without a clear knowledge of salvation. They have sometimes a "good hope" that they are saved, but then sin breaks out within them in such overwhelming power, that, thereby made to know the utter corruption of their sinful hearts, they are plunged back into uncertainty and distress. They are thus deprived of the fulness of the blessing which belongs to all who believe in Christ, owing to ignorance (oftentimes through bad teaching) of the two natures, and of the provision which God has made in Christ for indwelling sin, as well as for sins. In other words, they have never learned that complete deliverance is to be found in Christ, both from the guilt of sin and from our sinful nature, so that the believer can say, "There is therefore now no condemnation to them which are in Christ Jesus. . . . For the law of the Spirit of life in Christ Jesus hath made me free from the law of sin and death." (Rom. viii. 1-2.)

The truth on this subject is specially unfolded in the epistle to the Romans, from chapter v. to the end of chapter viii. This section has been described by another as follows: "Hitherto the great truth of the remission of the believer's sins has been fully set forth, closing with the blessed privileges which belong to the justified man, but still in that connection, the expiatory efficacy of the blood of Jesus, and this displayed in His resurrection. Precious as it all is, it is not everything the believer wants. *He may be miserable in the discovery of what he finds within himself;* and if he know not the truth that applies to his difficulties on this score, he is in danger of yielding to hardness on one side, or of bearing a burdened spirit of bondage on the other. *How many saints have never learnt the extent of their deliverance, and go mourning from day to day under efforts which they would be the first to confess unavailing against their inward corruption!* How many settle down callously balancing their faith in the forgiveness of their sins by the blood of Christ as a set-off against a plague which they suppose must needs be, and, of course, with no more power over it than those who are honestly, but in vain, struggling to get better. Neither the one nor the other understands the value to them of the sentence already executed on the old man in the cross, nor their own new place before God in

Christ risen from the dead. This it is the Spirit's object to unfold in what follows."

The sentences italicised in the above extract find a striking confirmation in chapter vii., where we have a quickened man, one who has been born again, not knowing his deliverance from law, struggling and groaning under the burden of his indwelling sin, so much so that he cries, " I am carnal, sold under sin " (*v.* 14); and again, " I delight in the law of God after the inward man: but I see another law in my members, warring against the law of my mind, and bringing me into captivity to the law of sin which is in my members. O wretched man that I am! who shall deliver me from the body of this death?" (*vv.* 22–24.) This is precisely the condition of many who are termed anxious souls. It is the felt contrariety of their state to all that they had longed for and hoped which leads them to doubt whether they are saved.

How then has God met this need of the soul? There can be only one answer to this question: it is in the death of Jesus Christ. For not only did He, as we have seen, bear our sins in His own body on the tree, but He was also *made sin* for us (2 Cor. v. 21); yea, "God sending His own Son in the likeness of sinful flesh, and for sin, *condemned sin in the flesh.*" (Romans viii. 3.)

The application of this truth is expounded in

Romans vi. Having shown in the previous chapter that "where sin abounded, grace did much more abound: that as sin hath reigned unto death, even so might grace reign through righteousness unto eternal life by Jesus Christ our Lord" (*vv.* 20–21), the apostle proceeds, "What shall we say then? Shall we continue in sin, that grace may abound? God forbid. How shall *we, that are dead to sin,* live any longer therein? Know ye not, that so many of us as *were baptized into Jesus Christ were baptized into His death?* Therefore we are buried with Him by baptism into death: that like as Christ was raised up from the dead by the glory of the Father, even so we also should walk in newness of life. For if we have been planted together in the likeness of His death, we shall be also [in the likeness] of [His] resurrection: *knowing this, that our old man is crucified with* [*Him*], that the body of sin might be destroyed (annulled), that henceforth we should not serve sin. *For he that is dead is freed*" (*justified*, in margin) "*from sin.*" (Rom. vi. 1–7.)

If now we give attention to the words which we have emphasized by italics, we shall understand the whole subject. (1.) We are here taught that we have part in Christ's death: we "were baptized into (or unto) His death;" "our old man is crucified with Him." (*vv.* 3–6.) This is on the principle of substitution, a principle which finds a striking illustration in the following familiar incident. During the days of Napoleon I., a young man was drawn as a soldier, but having some means, he purchased a substitute, who went in his stead to fight the battles of his country. The substitute was soon killed, and not long after a decree for another conscription was issued. It so happened that the same young man was drawn for the second time, but he pleaded that he was a dead man. When asked what he meant by such a plea, he answered that, since his substitute had been killed, he himself ought to be regarded as dead. The case, from its singularity, was carried before the courts of law, and, after examination and trial, it was ruled that the young man was dead before the law of conscription, on the ground of the death of his substitute. So with us, if we are believers in the Lord Jesus Christ. We can plead that we have died in the person of our Substitute, that in Him the whole judgment and condemnation due to our sin and sins have been borne and exhausted. (2.) We are consequently "dead to sin" (*v.* 2); and being dead, we are "freed (justified) from sin." (*v.* 7.) That is, our Adam nature—the seat of indwelling sin—our old man, has been judicially judged by God in the death of Christ; so that the penalty has already been paid, our doom so completely met, that before God we are regarded as judicially dead, and being dead we are justified from sin—cleared from all charge on account of it, completely delivered from it, through our death in the death of Christ.

The practical consequences of this truth are given in the succeeding verses. "Now if we be dead with Christ, we believe that we shall also live with Him: knowing that Christ being raised from the dead dieth no more; death hath no more dominion over Him. For in that He died, He died unto sin once: but in that He liveth, He liveth unto God. *Likewise reckon ye yourselves to be dead indeed unto sin, but alive unto God in*" (not through) "*Christ Jesus our Lord.* Let not sin therefore reign in your mortal body, that ye should obey it in the lusts thereof," etc. (*vv.* 8–12.) We are thus reminded, by implication at least, that we have part not only in the death of Christ, but also in Him as risen. "For if we be dead with Him, we believe that we shall also live with Him" (*v.* 8); and this is confirmed and enforced by the fact, that "in that He died, He died unto sin once: but in that He liveth, He liveth unto God." (*v.* 10.)

Then follow the practical exhortations.

1. We are to *reckon* ourselves dead to sin. The very terms of the exhortation indicate the truth; for if we were actually dead, we could not be told to reckon ourselves so. What we are then to do is *to take God's estimate of ourselves.* Having judged

us, as to our Adam nature, in the cross of Christ, He holds us as having met our judgment, and consequently to be dead in His sight. This is His judicial estimate of every believer as to the old man; and this judicial estimate is to be the estimate of our faith. What God declares we are to believe, and to believe spite of all appearances or experiences to the contrary; and since He holds us to have been crucified with Christ, we are to reckon ourselves dead to sin. This will explain many otherwise difficult expressions in the Scriptures. "I am" (or have been) "crucified with Christ." (Gal. ii. 20.) "If ye be dead" (or have died) "with Christ," etc. (Col. ii. 20); these, and all such, setting forth the truth here considered, that God regards all believers as having died with Christ, and therefore as having in Him borne the condemnation of sin. And this truth is to be our vantage-ground in the presence of temptation. We should remember in the presence of all solicitations to sin, that our old man has been crucified with Christ, that the body of sin might be destroyed, that henceforth we should *not serve sin*. (Rom. vi. 6.)

Thus our place before God determines our responsibility; and hence if I yield to sin, I contradict in fact that I have died with Christ; for sin argues, evidences one alive in the flesh and acting in the flesh. On the other hand, taking God's estimate of myself to be true for faith, I cannot let sin reign in my mortal body, that I should obey it in the lust thereof. I reckon myself to be dead to sin, and therefore delivered from it by the death of Christ; and thus my peace is undisturbed because I know that the flesh which I still have in me, and which, if not kept in the place of death, would break out at any moment in unbridled lusts, has already been judged, and condemned on the cross.

2. But we are also to reckon ourselves as alive unto God in Christ Jesus our Lord. This, as before said, implies our resurrection with Christ—although this truth is not here formally stated—because it is only as being in the risen Christ that we can be alive unto God. In the Colossians we find this aspect fully developed, the apostle making the fact of our being risen with Christ the ground of a practical appeal: "If ye then be risen with Christ, seek those things which are above, where Christ sitteth on the right hand of God. Set your affection on things above, not on things on the earth. For ye are dead" (or have died), "and your life is hid with Christ in God." (Col. iii. 1–3.) It is not only therefore that we have been crucified with Christ, but in Christ we passed through death; for "God hath raised us up together" with Christ. (Eph. ii. 6.) This was typified by the passage of the Israelites through

the Red Sea. In type "the Red Sea is evidently the death and resurrection of Jesus, and of His people *in Him;* God acting in it, in order to bring them into death to sin, and to deliverance from it, by death, where He had brought them *in Christ,* and consequently beyond the possibility of being reached by the enemy. We are made partakers of it already through faith. Sheltered from the judgment of God by the blood, we are delivered, by His power which acts for us, from the power of Satan, the prince of this world. The blood keeping us from the judgment of God was the beginning. The power which has made us alive, through Christ, has made us free from the whole power of Satan, who followed us, and from all his attacks and accusations. We have done with Egypt and the world."

> God who gave the blood to screen us,
>   God looks down in perfect love;
> Clouds may seem to pass between us,
>   There's no change in Him above.
>
> Though the restless foe accuses,
>   Sins recounting like a flood;
> Every charge our God refuses:
>   Christ hath answer'd with His blood.
>
> In the refuge God provided—
>   Though the world's destruction lowers—
> We are safe—to Christ confided,
>   Everlasting life is ours.

> And, ere long, when come to glory,
>   We shall sing a well-known strain,
> This—the never-tiring story,
>   "Worthy is the Lamb once slain!"

Two things have to be carefully noted. It is *in Christ* that we are alive unto God; and secondly, our being so is to be a matter of faith: we are to reckon ourselves so. We are alive in Christ really and actually; but this is not the thought here presented. We are also in this respect to take God's estimate, spite of all the contradictions to it within and without. Since God regards me as dead to sin, and alive unto Him in Christ Jesus, I am to reckon myself so; His estimate being the foundation of my faith and confidence, as well as the measure of my responsibility.

We are thus before God brought through the death and resurrection of Christ out of our old state and standing altogether, into a place and sphere where the flesh has no entrance—a deliverance so complete that not only is it said, "There is therefore now no condemnation to them which are in Christ Jesus," but also, "Ye are not in the flesh, but in the Spirit, if so be the Spirit of God dwell in you." (Rom. viii. 1, 9.) Such is our perfect standing before God in Christ as risen from the dead.

3. We shall now be in a position to understand the concluding exhortation of the passage cited;

viz., "Let not sin therefore reign in your mortal body, that ye should obey it in the lusts thereof." (Rom. vi. 12, etc.) We have here the contrast between our standing before God in Christ Jesus and our practical condition. He holds us, as we have seen, as dead to sin; but this exhortation supposes the presence of sin in the believer. Now it is in the understanding of this contrast, and its practical consequences and responsibilities, that the solution is found of the difficulties which are so often encountered at the outset of the Christian life, and which indeed in many cases keep believers in bondage for years, if not throughout the whole of their lives. It behoves us to be the more careful that our statements, in summing up the teachings upon this subject, are according to the word of God.

(α) Indwelling sin will always be present in the believer. Though he has a complete deliverance before God, the flesh in him remains unchanged; so that he will ever have to say, "In my flesh dwelleth no good thing." He must therefore never expect any amendment in the character of the flesh. What it was before his conversion it will be after, until he departs to be with Christ, either at His coming or through death. (Rom. vii. 18; viii. 1–13; Gal. iii. 16–26.)

(β) The presence of indwelling sin does not affect our perfect standing, our complete acceptance, before God in Christ Jesus; for God regards us as dead to sin. This is His judicial estimate of us, and consequently He looks upon the sin in us as already judged in the death of Christ. Thus sin in the flesh has been condemned. (Rom. viii. 3.) Its motions therefore within me, *if I do not yield to them,* cannot for one minute obscure even my enjoyment of the love of God; for I reckon the flesh in me as judged, according to His own estimate. It is thus not only that my standing is unalterable, but also my peace, my communion, is undisturbed. (γ) My responsibility is measured by God's estimate. If He regards me as dead to sin, I have to do the same; *and therefore I must not allow sin to reign in my mortal body, that I should obey it in the lusts thereof.* For if I were to allow sin to reign, I should practically contradict God's estimate of me as dead to it. I have thus to keep myself in the place of death, to mortify my members which are upon the earth (Col. iii. 5), because I am dead with Christ. Here then is the whole secret. I cannot rid myself of the foe. But God has judged it, and I have simply to act according to that judgment; to keep it in that place of death where He has already put it. Hence we are not told to expel sin, to root it out, to cast it away from us, as moralists, and even divines, ignorant of the Scriptures, sometimes exhort us to do; but we are told not to let it reign; *i.e.* it must be kept under, in the place and under the sentence of death which has been passed upon it.

"Ah!" you exclaim, "here is my difficulty. How am I, a poor feeble creature, to do this thing?" It is thus that unbelief ever speaks. Look at David in the presence of Goliath. Does he feel the impossibility of coping with such a powerful adversary? Nothing of the kind. His one conviction was that "the battle was the Lord's;" that Goliath was the Lord's enemy, and hence that the Lord would that day deliver him into his hand. (1.Sam. xvii. 45-47.) He thus measured his foe by the strength of the Lord; and by that measurement Goliath dwindled down before him into a puny dwarf, yea, into utter impotence and nothingness. So should it be with us. Granted that indwelling sin is strong and active, yet He who tells us to reckon ourselves to be dead to it, has supplied the power to enable us to comply with the exhortation. He has given us the indwelling Spirit, and if we "*through the Spirit* do mortify the deeds of the body, we shall live" (Rom. viii. 13); if "we walk in the Spirit, we shall not fulfil the lust of the flesh." (Gal. v. 16.) The Spirit of God is therefore our strength in this warfare, the all-sufficient power given to enable us to keep sin from reigning in our mortal body.

The completeness of our deliverance is thus not

even touched by the presence of indwelling sin. God has judged it in the death of Christ; we are brought clean out from under its power through the resurrection of Christ; and we have the power, in the Holy Spirit dwelling in our hearts, to keep it where God has put it, under judgment and death. Blessed be His name! We can therefore, like Israel, stand upon the resurrection side of our Red Sea, and sing, " The Lord is my strength and song, and He is become my salvation." (Exodus xv. 2.)

> "O Lord! Thou now art risen,
>   Thy travail all is o'er;
> For sin Thou once hast suffered—
>   Thou liv'st to die no more.
> Sin, death, and hell are vanquished
>   By Thee, the Church's Head;
> And, lo! we share Thy triumphs,
>   Thou First-born from the dead.
>
> "Into Thy death baptized,
>   We own with Thee we died;
> With Thee, our Life, we're risen,
>   And shall be glorified.
> From sin, the world, and Satan,
>   We're ransom'd by Thy blood;
> And here would walk as strangers,
>   Alive with Thee to God."

CHAPTER IX.

THE INDWELLING SPIRIT.

"YE are all the sons (υἱοί) of God by faith in Christ Jesus." (Gal. iii. 26.) "And because ye are sons, God has sent forth the Spirit of His Son into your hearts, crying, Abba, Father." (iv. 6.) This is the divine order. We are born of the Spirit through faith in Christ Jesus, and thus are made sons; then God sends forth the Spirit as the Spirit of sonship to dwell in our hearts. The indwelling of the Spirit is therefore, it will be observed, not coincident with, but consequent upon, becoming sons.

This divine order is shadowed forth in God's dealings with Israel. On the passover night, while still in Egypt, Israel was completely sheltered by the blood; but it is not until they had crossed the Red Sea that we read either of salvation, or of God's "holy habitation;" and we know that, as a matter of fact, God did not dwell in the midst of His people until they were brought out from Egypt, through the Red Sea, into the wilderness. So now. A soul may be quickened, born again, be under the protection of the blood of

Christ, but he must be indwelt by the Spirit of God before he can cry, "Abba, Father." (Gal. iv. 6.) Accordingly, we do not find in the epistle to the Romans any distinct mention of the Holy Spirit, as dwelling in the believer, until we come to the eighth chapter. As long as the believer does not know his deliverance from sin and from the law, we search in vain for any teaching on this subject; but no sooner do we get the complete answer to the question raised, "O wretched man that I am! who shall deliver me from the body of this death?" than we are told, "Ye are not in the flesh, but in the Spirit, *if so be that the Spirit of God dwell in you.*" (Romans viii. 9.)

The truth then is that every saved soul has the indwelling Spirit; and doubtless when the gospel was first proclaimed—proclaimed as it was in all its fulness, simplicity, and power—those who received it by the grace of God were brought at once out of darkness into light, and immediately received the seal of their redemption in the gift of the Holy Ghost. But now in the confusion that reigns around, when the gospel has been so largely corrupted by human admixtures, that the fulness of the grace of God in Christ Jesus is seldom preached, there are numbers who, though quickened, are still groping in the twilight, groaning in the house of their bondage, and consequently have not yet received that Spirit of adoption whereby alone believers can cry, Abba, Father. For "the Spirit itself beareth witness with our spirit, that we are the children of God" (Rom. viii. 16); and hence if we do not know that we are children of God, and cannot cry in filial confidence, Abba, Father, it is because we have not the Holy Ghost dwelling in us.

Our object now is to unfold what the Scriptures teach concerning this subject. As we have seen, the Spirit of God takes up His abode in us, consequent upon our becoming sons. And this it is which distinguishes a Christian from the saints under the old dispensation. Jewish believers were quickened, born again, but they knew nothing of God's Spirit as dwelling in them; "for the Holy Ghost was not yet, because that Jesus was not yet glorified." (John vii. 39.) He wrought by His power; for it was He who quickened the Jewish saints, as well as Christians; He also strengthened them for walk and service; but His coming down from heaven as a person to dwell in believers, and in the Church, was consequent upon the death, resurrection, and ascension of Christ. This difference is marked in one aspect very plainly by a prayer of the psalmist: "Cast me not away from thy presence; and *take not thy Holy Spirit from me.*" (Ps. li. 11); but the apostle Paul, writing to the Ephesians, says, "And grieve not the Holy Spirit of God, whereby *ye are sealed unto the day of redemption.*" (Eph. iv. 30.) Working by His influences in the heart of the psalmist, it was possible for him to lose that blessed power; but believers now, though they may grieve, are sealed by the Holy Spirit until the day of redemption. Just as the presence of the Holy Ghost upon the earth, in the house of God, characterises Christianity, so His dwelling in God's children distinguishes them from the believers of all past dispensations. For it is the Holy Spirit that unites us to Christ, makes us members of His body, of His flesh, and of His bones (1 Cor. xii. 13; Eph. v. 30); and this union, this place as members of His body, was not possible until Christ had been glorified, and had taken the place of Head in heaven.

There are several prominent aspects of the indwelling Spirit which we desire briefly to notice.

1. *As a witness.* The presence of the Holy Spirit on earth is the witness of accomplished redemption. For before our Lord departed, He promised to send "another Comforter" (John xiv. 16, 17, 25, 26; xv. 26, 27; xvi. 7–14); and He distinctly told His disciples that "He would send the promise of His Father upon them," and that they were to "tarry in Jerusalem until they were endued with power from on high." (Luke xxiv. 49.) The descent therefore of the

Holy Ghost on the day of Pentecost was the infallible sign of the completion of redemption, or rather the proof that God had accepted and was resting satisfied in the finished work of Christ. For "it is the Spirit that beareth witness, because the Spirit is truth." (1 John v. 6.)

But here we speak rather of the Spirit as dwelling in God's children, and as such, as we have seen, He "bears witness with our spirit, that we are the children of God." (Rom. viii. 15, 16; Gal. iv. 6, 7.) In this aspect, He is the witness of accomplished redemption to the individual soul—as will be seen when treating the next point—and hence every child of God ought to know by this sure testimony that he is saved. But it may be asked, How is this witness borne to our sonship? The very fact of His presence within us testifies to it; but by His presence He forms within us affections suited to our relationship, begets in us desires after the enjoyment of the Father's love, enables us in the holy intimacies of our filial place and position to cry, Abba, Father, verifies to our souls the word on which we have trusted as revealing to us the relationship and the blessings which belong to us as God's children, and thus bears very distinct witness with our spirit. No! it is not an audible testimony, and it is discerned and apprehended by our spirit alone; but it is none the less, nay, it is all the more, real on this account, because indeed it is a living secret between ourselves and God. The strength and distinctness of His testimony, it ought not to be forgotten, will depend upon conditions. "As many as are *led by* the Spirit of God, they are the sons of God." In other words, just as being led by the Spirit of God is an evidence of our being the sons of God, so it is, when we are led walking in simple, loving obedience and dependence, that our spirit will discern most clearly His testimony to our sonship. But if we are so walking as to grieve Him, we shall listen in vain for His testimony, for we shall have grieved Him into silence. God will not therefore permit any of His children to walk carelessly, resting the certainty of their salvation on the ground of their being children; but He reminds us that if we are His we shall be led of the Spirit, and that He will bear witness with our spirit, and teach us to cry, Abba, Father.

2. *As a Seal.* This truth is set before us in several passages. "Now He which stablisheth us with you in Christ, and hath anointed us, is God; who hath also *sealed* us." (2 Cor. i. 21, 22.) Again, "In whom also after that ye believed, ye were *sealed* with that Holy Spirit of promise." (Eph. i. 13); and in the same epistle we are exhorted to "grieve not the Holy Spirit of God, whereby ye are *sealed* unto the day of redemption." (iv. 30.) The Holy Spirit given to dwell in believers is

Himself the seal; *i.e.* God thereby marks them out, takes possession of them as His own, and declares them by the Spirit being within them to be His property. If one may use the illustration, just as the broad-arrow declares the thing on which it is marked to belong to the Queen, so the Spirit of God sets us apart, marks us out as belonging to God. But the figure is that of a seal. Now the seal not only indicated ownership by the impress upon it, but it was put also for protection. Hence believers are said to be sealed until the day of redemption. They are secured by the seal until the Lord shall return to receive them unto Himself. And hence only believers are sealed; and they are not sealed until they are the Lord's, until they are brought out of the house of their bondage (as before seen), through the death and resurrection of Christ, until they not only are safe, but are also saved.

3. *As an Earnest.* Two of the passages already cited speak of the Spirit as the earnest. "Who hath also sealed us, and given *the earnest* of the Spirit in our hearts" (2 Cor. i. 22); "In whom after that ye believed, ye were sealed with that Holy Spirit of promise, which is *the earnest* of our inheritance until the redemption of the purchased possession, unto the praise of His glory." (Eph. i. 13, 14.) It is the latter passage which defines most exactly the character of the earnest. The Holy

Spirit as now given is regarded as "the earnest of our inheritance;" that is, He is the first-fruits of that which we shall inherit in and through the Lord Jesus Christ. As indeed when a sale is effected of a property, a portion of the purchase-money is paid down as *earnest*-money for the completion of the bargain, so God graciously gives us the indwelling Spirit as the earnest of our inheritance, thereby assuring us that we shall possess all that He has promised, and binding Himself (if we may so speak) to accomplish His own faithful word; for the earnest-money is both a promise and a pledge. But the Holy Spirit is even more, because, as we have seen, He is also the seal, thereby securing us for the inheritance, as well as certifying us that God will put us into possession of it to the praise of His glory.

4. It would lead us far beyond the scope of these pages to enter fully upon the offices of the indwelling Spirit. We can therefore only briefly indicate that He alone is our power for worship (John iv. 23, 24; Phil. iii. 3); for prayer (Rom. viii. 26, 27; Eph. vi. 18; Jude 20); for walk (Rom. viii. 14; Gal. v. 16-26); for service (1 Cor. ii. 4; 1 Thess. i. 5, etc.); for the apprehension of truth (1 Cor. ii. 9-16; John xvi. 13; 1 John ii. 20-27); for growth (Eph. iii. 16-19), etc. Indeed, as the Spirit characterizes our existence before God—for we are not in the flesh, but in the Spirit,

if so be that the Spirit of God dwell in us (Rom. viii. 2)—He only is the source of power for all the activities of our spiritual life, whether those activities have God or man for their object. Blessed fact! for it is only when we know our own weakness and nothingness that we can learn the lesson of dependence; and when we are dependent, the Spirit of God is free to act within us according to His will.

A caution is often given, and much needed both by anxious souls and young believers, not to confound the Spirit's work *in* us with Christ's work *for* us. Thus another has said, "We are constantly prone to look at something in ourselves as necessary to form the ground of peace. We are apt to regard the work of the Spirit *in* us, rather than the work of Christ *for* us, as the foundation of our peace. This is a mistake. . . . The Holy Ghost did not make peace; but Christ did. The Holy Ghost is not said to be our peace; but Christ is. God did not send 'preaching peace.' by the Holy Ghost, but 'by Jesus Christ.' (Compare Acts x. 36; Eph. xi. 14, 17; Col. i. 20.) The Holy Ghost reveals Christ; He makes us know, enjoy, and feed upon Christ. He bears witness to Christ, takes of the things of Christ, and shows them unto us. He is the power of communion, the seal, the witness, the earnest, the unction. In short, His operations are essential.

Without Him we can neither see, hear, know, feel, experience, enjoy, nor exhibit aught of Christ. This is plain, and is understood and admitted by every true and rightly-instructed Christian. Yet, notwithstanding all this, the work of the Spirit is not the ground of peace, though He enables us to enjoy the peace. He is not our title, though He reveals our title, and enables us to enjoy it." No; the foundation or ground of peace is Christ —Christ in His finished work which He accomplished on the cross. For whoever believes " on Him that raised up Jesus our Lord from the dead, who was delivered for our offences, and was raised again for our justification," is justified; and " being justified by faith, *we have peace with God through our Lord Jesus Christ.*" (Rom. iv. 24, 25; v. 1.) The foundation of peace then, it should ever be remembered, is outside of ourselves; and the indwelling of the Holy Spirit, as pointed out, is consequent upon our becoming the sons of God.

But we cannot be too sensible to the fact that, if believers, we have the Spirit of God dwelling in us; nor too solicitous not to grieve Him by unholy actings in the flesh. (See Ephes. iv. 29–32.) Hence too the solemn interrogation of the apostle, "What? know ye not that your body is the temple of the Holy Ghost [which is] in you, which ye have of God, and ye are not your own? For ye are bought with a price: therefore glorify God in

THE INDWELLING SPIRIT.

your body" (1 Cor. vi. 19, 20); and the exhortations, "Walk in the Spirit, and ye shall not fulfil the lust of the flesh;" "If we live in the Spirit, let us also walk in the Spirit." (Gal. v. 16–25.)

> "What moved Thee to impart
> Thy Spirit from above,
> Therewith to fill our heart
> With heavenly peace and love?
> 'Twas love, unbounded love to us,
> Moved Thee to give Thy Spirit thus."

> "The Comforter, now present,
> Assures us of Thy love;
> He is the blessèd earnest
> Of glory there above:
> The river of Thy pleasure
> Is what sustains us now;
> Till Thy new name's imprinted
> On every sinless brow."

> "Thou hast bestow'd the earnest
> Of that we shall inherit;
> Till Thou shalt come to take us home,
> We're sealed by God the Spirit.
> We wait for Thine appearing,
> When we shall know more fully
> The grace divine that made us Thine,
> Thou Lamb of God most holy!"

CHAPTER X.

STANDING AND RESPONSIBILITY.

No exposition of the salvation which is connected with faith in Christ would be complete, without some explanation of the perfect place of blessing into which we are thereby brought. There is little doubt indeed that many quickened souls are also kept in the bondage of doubt and anxiety through their ignorance of what Christ has really accomplished on their behalf; and it is perfectly certain that they can have no adequate apprehension of their responsibility without a knowledge of their position in Christ Jesus.

Every one understands that forgiveness of sins is the immediate portion of the believer in Christ. But great as is this blessing, it is but a small part of the provisions of grace. "Being justified by faith, we have peace with God through our Lord Jesus Christ." (Rom. v. 1.) The very next verse speaks of two additional blessings: "access by faith into this grace in which we stand," *i.e.* into the full favour of God in Christ; and "rejoicing in hope of the glory of God," *i.e.* the full fruition and consummation of our present blessings. But these gifts of God's grace through Christ belong to us here, as justified men; and in the same way we can turn to other passages which speak of perfect and everlasting reconciliation. (See Col. i. 21, 22.) But there is something beyond all this; as indeed we partly saw when treating of "deliverance."

What then is our standing, position, or place before God? It is in Christ where He is. Let us explain. We have seen (chap. viii.) that every believer is regarded by God as having died with Christ; that the apostle could write to the Colossians, "Ye are dead, and your life is hid with Christ in God" (Col. iii. 3); and the context (*v.* 1) of the same passage speaks further of our "being risen with Christ." Turning to another epistle we get even more. "But God, who is rich in mercy, for His great love wherewith He loved us, even when we were dead in sins, hath quickened us together with Christ, (by grace ye are saved;) and hath raised us up together, *and made us sit together in heavenly places in Christ Jesus.*" (Eph. ii. 4–6.) These expressions refer to something already accomplished, and we learn from them that, though we are still actually in the body on the earth, we are before God seated in heavenly places in Christ Jesus; that the work of Christ on our behalf is so efficacious and wonderful, so God-glorifying, that God even now can righteously accord us a position in Christ in the heavenly places. For Christ "has not only borne our sins, and died to sin, and closed the whole history of the old man in death, for those who believe, they having been crucified with Him; but He has glorified God in this work (John xiii. 31, 32; xvii. 4, 5), and so obtained a place for man in the glory of God, and a place of present positive acceptance, according to the nature and favour of God whom He has glorified; and that is our place before God. It is not only that the old man and his sins are all put out of God's sight, *but we are in Christ before God.*" Every believer therefore has been crucified with Christ, raised up with Him, and is now seated in Him in the heavenlies. He is thus taken altogether out of his old standing—his Adam standing; for "he is not in the flesh but in the Spirit, if so be the Spirit of God dwell in him (Rom. viii. 9); and his new standing is in Christ, and thus of necessity in Christ where He is. Hence too the measure of His acceptance is the acceptance of Christ; "for as He is so are we in this world." (1 John iv. 17.)

This is often very difficult for the young believer to understand. Be it therefore very distinctly noted that it is no question whatever of attainment or experience, that it belongs to every believer; and the difficulty will vanish if the eye be taken off from self and directed to Christ. If we look within, consider our weaknesses, failures, imperfections, sins, well might we be perplexed to understand how such imperfect ones, as we are practically, could have such a perfect and inalienable place before God. But when we look at Christ, at His precious blood, at what He was to God on the cross, and what He accomplished there, we instantly confess that He is worthy of the place He fills. Here is the whole secret. It is in His worthiness we stand. All that we were, as to the old nature, is gone from before God: Christ only remains, and we in Him. Our place, standing, is thus God's response to the worthiness, the merits, of His own Son. He can therefore righteously shelter us by the blood, bring us out of Egypt, through the Red Sea, across the Jordan, and set us down in Christ in the heavenlies.

And just because our standing is in Christ, it is unalterable and immutable. Knowing this, the completeness of our redemption, because of our union with that blessed One who is risen from among the dead, we have abiding confidence and peace. *We* may change, fluctuate in feeling and attainment, but Christ can never change; He is "the same yesterday, and to-day, and for ever." (Heb. xiii. 8.) And hence, since our standing is in Him, we dwell for ever in the light and presence of God; for our home is before Him, though we may sometimes forget it; and where should we dwell but in our home? The more fully therefore we understand our true place and standing in Christ, the more familiar shall we be with the presence and glory of God.

But such a wondrous place or standing has its *responsibilities;* and it is to these we would now turn. As we have seen, we are in Christ before God; and, marvellous fact, Christ is in us down here (see John xv. 4; Gal. ii. 20; Eph. iii. 17; Col. i. 27, etc.), and this defines and measures our responsibilities; for if God has given us a place in Christ where He is, it is that we may exhibit Christ where we are. A few illustrations of this may be collected from the Scriptures. "He that saith he abideth in Him ought himself also so to *walk, even as He walked.*" (1 John ii. 6.) Taking this in its most general form, we may ask, And how did the Lord Jesus walk? Ever as the heavenly One upon the earth. As when speaking to Nicodemus, He could say, "The Son of man which is in heaven" (John iii. 13), so was it during the whole of His earthly sojourn; for the life He lived was a heavenly life—as One who had come forth from the Father, revealing Him, and unfolding the perfectness of heaven upon earth. He could thus say, "He that hath seen me hath seen the Father" (John xiv. 9); for morally He was the perfect presentation of the Father. So ought we to walk—as belonging not to earth, but to heaven, and unfolding the ways of heaven upon earth—as samples of the heavenly character; for we are dead with Christ. We have not only died in Him to sin, but we have also died with Him from out of this scene in which we move, and have been raised together with Him. Our citizenship, or commonwealth, is in heaven (Phil. iii. 20), and in accordance with this character must be our lives. This responsibility is summed up, in its double aspect, by the apostle Paul when he says, "Always bearing about in the body the dying of the Lord Jesus, that the life also of Jesus might be made manifest in our body. For we which live are alway delivered unto death for Jesus' sake, that the life also of Jesus might be made manifest in our mortal flesh." (2 Cor. iv. 10, 11.) Thus it is death on the one side, and life on the other: death as to all that we were in the flesh; life as to all that we are in Christ, or rather, Christ Himself as our life—manifested even in our mortal flesh. Hence the obligation to mortify our members which are upon the earth (Col. iii. 5)—an obligation which distinctly flows from the fact that our standing is in Christ risen. The apostle shows that he had apprehended the responsibility when he says, "To me to live is Christ" (Phil. i. 21); and just in proportion as we approximate to the ability to say the same thing will be our understanding of our true place in Christ.

Another form of our responsibility is found in the passage, " Be ye therefore followers (imitators) of God, as dear children; *and walk in love, as Christ also hath loved us,* and hath given Himself for us an offering and a sacrifice to God for a sweet-smelling savour." (Eph. v. 1, 2.) The same thing is enforced by the apostle John. Herein we have known love, because He has laid down His life for us: and *we* ought to lay down our lives for the brethren. (1 John iii. 16.) We have also an example, in one particular direction, given in John xiii. After the Lord Jesus had washed the feet of His disciples, "and had taken His garments, and was set down again, He said unto them, Know ye what I have done to you? Ye call me Master and Lord: and ye say well; for so I am. If I then, [your] Lord and Master, have washed your feet; ye also ought to wash one another's feet. For I have given you an example, that ye should do as I have done to you." (John xiii. 12–15.) The love of Christ therefore to us, even in yielding Himself up to death on our behalf, is proposed to us as our example. If He laid down His life for us, we ought to lay down our lives for the brethren, love's uttermost expression, and this—no degree short of this—is our responsibility.

But mark the language of the first of the passages which we have cited; and see how carefully the Spirit of God has defined the character of the love which should also flow out from us, and thereby guarded it from degenerating into human kindness and amiability. It is, "As Christ also hath loved us, and hath given Himself for us *an offering and a sacrifice to God for a sweet-smelling savour.*" While therefore we are under responsibility to love our brethren to the uttermost, God, and not they, is to be the object before our souls. It must be expressed as to Him; and can therefore only be expressed in the pathways of obedience. "By this we know that we love the children of God, when we love God, and keep His commandments." (1 John v. 2.) Accordingly, our Lord's sacrifice of Himself is characterised as "obedience unto death" (Phil. ii. 8); and He Himself thus speaks of it: "I have power to lay it" (His life) "down, and I have power to take it again. This *commandment* have I received of my Father." (John x. 18.) Thus Christ must be before our souls—Christ in motive as well as act, in treading in His path of love, in seeking to love one another, even as He hath loved us. (John xv. 12.)

The apostle Peter gives us another aspect of our responsibility in the presentation of Christ in walk, an aspect towards enemies or persecutors. "If, when ye do well, and suffer [for it], ye take it patiently, this is acceptable with God. For even hereunto were ye called: because Christ also suffered for us, leaving us an example, that ye should follow His steps: who did no sin, neither was guile found in His mouth: who, when He was reviled, reviled not again; when He suffered, He threatened not; but committed Himself to Him that judgeth righteously: who His own self bare our sins in His own body on the tree, that we, being dead to sins, should live unto righteousness: by whose stripes ye were healed." (1 Peter ii. 20–24.) It is thus Christ, in whatever way we look; for since He is our life, our responsibility is to live Christ. "I am crucified with Christ: nevertheless I live; yet not I, but Christ liveth in me: and the life which I now live in the flesh I live by the faith of the Son of God, who loved me, and gave Himself for me." (Gal. ii. 20.)

It may tend to simplify the whole subject, and aid in its apprehension, if we refer briefly to two other passages which treat of it in another form. Ephesians iv. 20–32, and Colossians iii. contain a number of practical exhortations which are all based upon our standing in Christ. We take the latter to indicate their general character. The first part of the chapter (Col. iii.) deals with our death and resurrection with Christ, on which we have already touched. Following upon this we have practical directions. Then the apostle lays the foundation of all. "Lie not one to another, *seeing that ye have put off the old man with his deeds; and have put on the new* [*man*]*,* which is renewed in knowledge after the image of Him that created him: where there is neither Greek nor Jew, circumcision nor uncircumcision, Barbarian, Scythian, bond [nor] free: *but Christ is all, and in all.* Put on therefore, as the elect of God, holy and beloved, bowels of mercies, kindness," etc. (Col. iii. 9–12.) Without entering upon a detailed exposition of the passage, it will be observed that the ground of the exhortations lies in the Colossian believers having "put off the old man," and having "put on the new." But when did they put off the old man? It was in the death of Christ that our old man (Adam) was crucified. (Rom. vi. 6.) And when did they put on the new man? In the resurrection of Christ. (Col. ii. 11–13; iii. 1–5.) And herein lies the whole of our responsibility. For if I, through grace, have put off the old man, my responsibility is, to live no longer according to the old man, but to mortify my members which are upon the earth; and if I have put on the new man, I am under the obligation to walk accordingly, For we have been brought, through the death and resurrection of Christ, out of the old state and standing in which Adam was all and in all, into the new, where Christ is all and in all. If therefore Christ in glory is the measure of my standing, He also is the measure of my responsibility, and these two things are always connected in the word of God, as they should also ever be connected in our own souls. "If any man be in Christ, a new creature" (2 Cor. v. 17), *i.e.* he is brought into that new creation of which Christ is the beginning and the Head; and hence every believer is responsible to walk in accordance with the **character of the place into which he is brought.**

"O Lord! when we the path retrace
 Which Thou on earth hast trod,
To man Thy wondrous love and grace,
 Thy faithfulness to God;

' Thy love, by man so sorely tried,
 Proved stronger than the grave;
The very spear that pierced Thy side
 Drew forth the blood to save;

Faithful amidst unfaithfulness,
 'Mid darkness only light,
Thou didst Thy Father's name confess,
 And in His will delight;

Unmoved by Satan's subtle wiles,
 Or suffering, shame, and loss,
Thy path, uncheered by earthly smiles,
 Led only to the cross:—

We wonder at Thy lowly mind,
 And fain would like Thee be,
And all our rest and pleasure find
 In learning, Lord, of Thee."

CHAPTER XI.

THE COMING OF THE LORD.

ONE object of hope is placed before the believer in the Scriptures as soon as he has been brought out of darkness into God's marvellous light, and that is the coming or return of the Lord Jesus. This is the case in almost every book of the New Testament; and this fact makes it the more surprising that the hope of the Lord's return has been lost sight of by almost the whole professing Church. Let us examine the Scriptures on this point.

In the first place, we shall find that our Lord Himself was continually pressing this truth upon the attention of His disciples. In the gospel of Matthew it is found again and again, and the "parable of the virgins" embodies it in its most striking form. (Matt. xxv.) In Mark we get the exhortation, "Watch ye therefore: for ye know not when the Master of the house cometh, at even, or at midnight, or at the cock-crowing, or in the morning," etc. (xiii. 35–37.) In Luke we read, "Let your loins be girded about, and your lights burning; and ye yourselves like unto men that wait for their lord, when he will return from the wedding; that when he cometh and knocketh, they may open unto him immediately." (xii. 35, 36.) In John we have those blessed and familiar words: "Let not your heart be troubled: ye believe in God, believe also in me. In my Father's house are many mansions: if [it were] not [so], I would have told you. I go to prepare a place for you. And if I go and prepare a place for you, *I will come again, and receive you unto myself; that where I am, [there] ye may be also.*" (xiv. 1-3.)

These are only samples of the way in which the Lord presented His return to His disciples; and we now pass on to the subsequent books of the New Testament, because it is after the resurrection and ascension of Christ that the Holy Spirit reveals this truth as the distinctive hope of the believer. Indeed, no sooner had the Lord been taken from His disciples up into heaven than this message was sent to them: "Ye men of Galilee, why stand ye gazing up into heaven? *this same Jesus, which is taken up from you into heaven, shall so come in like manner as ye have seen Him go into heaven.*" (Acts i. 10, 11.) Passing still onward to the epistles which were addressed to churches or to saints, we shall find the same thing. The first epistle to the Thessalonians was the earliest in point of time of these; and in this, describing their conversion, the apostle says:

"They themselves show of us what manner of entering in we had unto you, and how ye turned to God from idols to serve the living and true God; *and to wait for His Son from heaven.*" (1 Thess. i. 9, 10; see also ii. 19, 20; iii. 13; iv. 13–18, etc.) The second epistle to the same church treats of the same subject, correcting some mistakes into which the saints were in danger of falling through false teaching. (See 2 Thess. ii. 1–6.) In Colossians we have the same distinct note—" When Christ, [who is] our life, shall appear, then shall ye also appear with Him in glory" (iii. 4), showing here indeed that the saints will have been caught up to meet the Lord before His appearing. In Philippians also we have, " Our conversation is in heaven; from whence also we look for the Saviour, the Lord Jesus Christ." (iii. 20.) So in Titus, " Looking for that blessed hope, and the glorious appearing of the great God and our Saviour Jesus Christ." (ii. 13.)

Taking now the last book of the Bible, what do we find? The same thing both at the commencement and at the close. Of all the seven churches Philadelphia seems most in accord with the Lord's mind; and it is to it that He says, " Behold, I come quickly: hold that fast which thou hast, that no man take thy crown." (Rev. iii. 11.) And our Lord thus closes His communications to His people, and the whole canon of inspired truth: " He which testifieth these things saith, Surely I come quickly" (Rev. xxii. 20), sufficient evidence surely of the place He would have His coming to occupy in our minds.

And not only is it the fact that our attitude should ever be that of waiting for the Lord Jesus, but we are also taught that there is nothing of necessity, as far as is revealed, between the present and that coming, no intervening events to occupy us or to turn aside our gaze; but that at any moment, even while this page is being written or read, the Lord may "descend from heaven with a shout, with the voice of the archangel, and with the trump of God," to raise His sleeping saints, and to change the living ones, that both alike may be caught up "in the clouds, to meet the Lord in the air." (1 Thess. iv. 15-18.) Thus the apostle, in the constant expectation of this event, says, "*We which are alive* and remain shall be caught up," etc. (*v.* 17); and again, "*We* shall not all sleep, but *we* shall be changed." (1 Cor. xv. 51.) Accordingly, it is the evil servant who is spoken of as saying in his heart, "My lord *delayeth his coming*" (Matt. xxiv. 48); and Peter also tells us that there will be scoffers in the last days, "walking after their own lusts, and saying, Where is the promise of His coming?" (2 Peter iii. 3, 4.)

Waiting, looking for, expecting the coming of the Lord should thus characterize every believer.

For, as we have continually seen in these pages, we are a heavenly people, and hence our hope is also heavenly; and we wait for the Lord Jesus, because He Himself has told us to do so. And, moreover, He has been pleased to reveal to us that then will be the consummation of our redemption. It is then that we shall be like Him (1 John iii. 2); that we shall be like Him bodily as well as morally. (Phil. iii. 21.) For if we shall have died as to the body ere He returns, He will raise us from among the dead, in resurrection bodies like His own; if we are still on the earth, we shall "be changed, in a moment, in the twinkling of an eye, at the last trump: for the trumpet shall sound, and the dead shall be raised incorruptible, and we" (*i.e.* the living) "shall be changed." (1 Cor. xv. 51, 52.) Then, too, not only shall we enter upon our association with Him in the glory, but we shall also "ever be with the Lord." (1 Thess. iv. 17.)

The effect of this hope upon the soul should be most blessed. We may adduce a few instances of the practical power which it is intended to exercise. Beyond all, the constant expectation of Christ constitutes a searching test of our spiritual condition. This is one of the main points in the parable of the virgins. (Matt. xxv. 1-13.) All the virgins are professors; but the fatal distinction is, that while five are wise, five are foolish. All alike had lamps, and all alike professed to go forth to meet the Bridegroom. Outwardly therefore there was no difference; and as far as can be discovered from the parable the essential difference between them was not detected until the cry was raised, "Behold the Bridegroom!" Then it is, in the prospect of His approach, and in order to be ready to meet Him, that they are aroused from their slumbers, and that they begin to trim their lamps; but no sooner was the light applied to the wicks of their lamps than five discover their lack of oil. Until now they had thought that all was well. They were professors, and walked, outwardly at least, as the Lord's people; but now, in the near prospect of meeting the Lord, they are made to know that they had no oil, that they had not been born again, that they had no indwelling Spirit to bear witness with their spirits that they were God's children, that they were professors and nothing else, and therefore that as such they could not meet the Bridegroom. Hence their endeavours to get the oil: but no, their efforts are vain; it is too late, for the Bridegroom and those that were ready have gone in to the marriage: "and the door was shut." (*v.* 10.) Undaunted still, they press onwards and reach the door, and standing there, they raise the pleading cry, "Lord, Lord, open to us. But He answered and said, Verily I say unto you, I know you not." (*vv.* 11, 12.) And the solemn lesson which the Lord Himself draws is this, "Watch therefore, for ye know neither the day nor the hour" (*v.* 13); for what happened to the foolish virgins in the parable may happen to any of us, if we take only the lamp of profession, and have no oil; *i.e.* if we are Christians only in name, never having been born again, and received the Spirit of adoption.

But not only does the expectation of Christ reveal the true state of professors, but it also discovers the condition of the wise virgins. These equally with the foolish had slumbered and slept, and it is the cry, "Behold the Bridegroom" which also awakens them, and constrains them to trim their lamps that they might go forth and meet Him; and it is only thus that being ready they went in with Him to the marriage. (*v.* 10.) Indeed, when believers are constantly expecting their Lord, it is impossible for them to sleep. In spirit they are already in His presence, and their own state and associations are instantly revealed. And it would seem from the parable that there are four things which constitute readiness to meet the Lord: First, the one essential thing, oil; secondly, the lamp trimmed and burning; thirdly, separation, for they were to *go out* to meet the Bridegroom; and lastly, watchfulness, for their failure was in having slumbered and slept. And it is when the Lord is momentarily expected that believers will seek to have these characteristics of preparedness for His presence.

It should be also an incentive to fidelity in service. Thus in the parable of the ten pounds, the charge which accompanied their delivery to the ten servants was, "Occupy till I come." (Luke xix. 12–27.) Concerning the evil servant, already mentioned, it is said, "The lord of that servant shall come in a day when he looketh not for him, and in an hour that he is not aware of, and shall cut him asunder, and appoint him his portion with the hypocrites," etc. (Matt. xxiv. 50, 51.) Thus the coming of Christ is a double motive to fidelity; it holds out encouragement to the faithful, and it affords a warning to the careless servant. The former will say with joyful anticipation, "My Lord is at hand, and therefore I must seek to be diligent ere He comes;" while the latter, if he reflect at all, will surely think, "What will my Lord say if He find me, at His coming, both careless and unfaithful?" The more fully therefore we live in the power of the expectation of Christ, the more shall we feel the need of serving as in His sight, knowing that He will reckon with us on His return.

The prospect of the coming of Christ exerts also a separating power upon heart and life. The apostle John says, "Beloved, now are we the sons of God, and it doth not yet appear what we shall be: but we know that when He shall appear we shall be like Him, for we shall see Him as He is. And every man that hath this hope in Him (*i.e.* in Christ) purifieth himself, even as He is pure." (1 John ii. 2, 3.) Nothing indeed will detach us from all that is unsuited to His presence like the constant expectation of Christ. Knowing that He may return at any moment, and living with this expectation, it will be our desire to be separated from all, whether in heart, manner, habit, life, and walk, on which He could not smile. Yea, it will lead us to judge everything within and without ourselves by the light of His presence as being in spirit already with Him, and thus having Him in glory continually before our souls, to "purify ourselves even as He is pure."

These are only some of the practical effects of the living expectation of the coming of Christ. If the Scriptures are examined further on the subject, it will be found that the coming of Christ is always associated with the heart and life of the believer. But enough has been said to indicate the practical character of the doctrine. A grievous wrong is therefore done to the young believer when he is kept in ignorance of this most blessed truth. For if the cross of Christ is the foundation, the coming of Christ is the completion of his salvation, for it is then, as we have seen, that in body also he will be like his Lord. And not only so, but he is also deprived of that hope which, applied by the Holy Spirit, not only sustains him in discouragement, comforts him in trouble, consoles him in bereavement, nerves him for conflict, stimulates his zeal, and calls forth his affections, but also works mightily for his practical sanctification. It is no wonder therefore that Satan should seek to obscure it from the minds of believers; but it is a wonder that so many should fall into his snare, inasmuch as our blessed Lord has for ever associated it with the touching memorials of His own death. For every time "we eat the bread, and drink the cup, we do show the Lord's death TILL HE COME." (1 Cor. xi. 26.)

> "'A little while!' the Lord shall come,
>   And we shall wander here no more;
> He'll take us to His Father's home,
>   Where He for us is gone before:
> To dwell with Him, to see His face,
> And sing the glories of His grace.
>
> "'A little while!" He'll come again:
>   Let us the precious hours redeem;
> Our only grief to give Him pain,
>   Our joy to serve and follow Him:
> Watching and ready may we be,
> As those that wait their Lord to see."

CHAPTER XII.

THE JUDGMENT.

Much confusion exists in the minds both of believers and unbelievers as to the judgment. The general idea is that at the end of the world there will be a judgment-day, when all alike, whether saved or unsaved, will stand before God, and receive according to their works. Hence it is often contended that we cannot know whether we are saved before that time. We therefore propose to examine this subject by the light of the Scriptures.

1. It is very certain that believers will never be judged—will never stand before the judgment-seat on account of sin. Our Lord teaches this doctrine most distinctly. He says, "Verily, verily, I say unto you, He that heareth my word, and believeth on Him that sent me, hath everlasting life, and shall not come into *condemnation;* but is passed from death unto life." (John v. 24.) Now this word "condemnation" should be translated *judgment*, and is so translated in verses 22, 27, and 29; and we have therefore a distinct assertion that

believers will not come into judgment. Indeed, this is only a simple consequence of having eternal life; for if the question of our state before God were left unsettled, how could we be possessors of everlasting life? And yet we are taught that we have this now: "He that heareth my word, and believeth on Him that sent me, *hath*" (not shall have) "everlasting life." (See also John iii. 36; vi. 47; 1 John v. 13, etc.)

This truth was shadowed forth in the distinction which God made between Israel and Egypt on the Passover night, when He smote the first-born. Israel, as we have seen, was completely sheltered from the power of the destroying angel, by the blood of the Lamb. In like manner every believer is secured from judgment as to guilt, by the blood of Christ; for Christ has borne the judgment for him in His death on the cross, so that he can say, "He bare my sins in His own body on the tree." (1 Peter ii. 24.)

"Yes," you may perhaps reply, "my past sins." "No," we answer, "your sins; all your sins if you are a believer. For not one of them had been committed when the Saviour died; and so He took the burden of all of them, entered into and exhausted the judgment due to all of them, so that the whole of your guilt might for ever be swept away. Blessed truth!"

> "If thou hast my discharge procured,
> And freely in my place endured
> The whole of wrath divine,
> Payment He will not twice demand,
> First at my bleeding surety's hand,
> And then again at mine."

Thus it is that we have not only died, but have also been raised together with Christ (Eph. ii.; Col. iii.), and therefore have been brought through the judgment, in the death of Christ, so that we stand on the other, the resurrection side, where in perfect confidence we can cry, "Who shall lay anything to the charge of God's elect? It is God that justifieth. Who is he that condemneth?" (Rom. viii. 33, 34.)

2. Though believers will never be judged on account of sin, all must appear before the judgment-seat of Christ. Thus the apostle writes: "We are confident [I say] and willing rather to be absent from the body, and to be present with the Lord. Wherefore we labour (or, it is our earnest desire), that, whether present or absent, we may be accepted of Him (or, acceptable to Him). *For we must all appear before the judgment-seat of Christ;* that every one may receive the things [done] in [his] body, according to that he hath done, whether [it be] good or bad." (2 Cor. v. 8–10.) No statement could be plainer to the effect that all, "*we* all," and therefore believers, must also appear before the judgment-seat of

Christ. We ask them these two questions: first, When will this be for believers? and secondly, For what purpose will they be there?

(a) When will believers appear before the judgment-seat of Christ? It has been seen in the previous chapter that the hope of the believer is the coming of Christ; and that at His coming the dead in Christ will be raised, that those who are living will be changed, and that both will be caught up together in the clouds to meet the Lord in the air. (1 Thess. iv. 16–18.) This applies to believers alone, and is "the resurrection of life" of which our Lord speaks in the gospel of John. If we cite the whole passage the reference will be better understood. He says, "The hour is coming in the which all that are in the graves shall hear His voice, and shall come forth; they that have done good, unto the resurrection of life; and they have done evil, unto the resurrection of damnation" (judgment, κρίσεως). (John v. 28, 29.) In verse 24, He proclaims everlasting life to every one that heareth His word, and believeth on Him that sent Him; and declares that all such shall not come into judgment, but are passed from death unto life. He then proceeds, "Verily, verily, I say unto you, The hour is coming, and now is, when the dead shall hear the voice of the Son of God: and they that hear shall live." He grounds this assurance upon the fact that "as the Father hath life in Himself, so hath He given to the Son to have life in Himself; and hath given Him authority to execute judgment also, because He is the Son of man." (*vv.* 25-27.) Then comes our passage, "Marvel not at this: for the hour is coming," etc. (*v.* 28.)

The two things here contrasted are life and judgment, in connection with Christ as the source of one, and the depositary of the other. As the Son of God He communicates life; as the Son of man He is invested with the authority to execute judgment. Accordingly He offers life in the hour that now is; and will execute judgment in the hour that is coming. The hour that "now is" has lasted therefore from the time when these words were spoken, and will last until the close of the present dispensation. Thus the dead in verse 25 are the spiritually dead; and hence we have the words "*they that hear* shall live;" for it is only they that hear the voice of the Son of God in the gospel who pass from death unto life. But in the coming hour (*v.* 28) we are told that *all that are in the graves* shall come forth; "the hour" in this case, as in verse 25, marking a period or dispensation, and therefore in no way indicating a simultaneous resurrection. On the other hand, as we know from other Scriptures (1 Cor. xv. 23; 1 Thess. iv. 15-18; Rev. xx. 4-6, etc.), the resurrection of life will take place at the Lord's return, while the resurrection of judgment will not be until the close of the millennium, being the closing event of earthly dispensations preparatory to the eternal state. What we get then from this passage is, that the resurrection of life of those who have heard the word of the Son of God, and believed on Him that sent Him, and have received everlasting life, is an entirely distinct thing from the resurrection of judgment; that believers have no part in the resurrection of judgment, and hence that they will not appear before the judgment-seat together with the wicked. There is also the other solemn instruction which we note and leave, as outside our present purpose, that all men must honour the Son of God, if not now by bowing before Him in self-judgment to receive everlasting life, then by-and-by when He executes judgment as the Son of man upon every one according to their works. Now He acts in grace; then in righteous judgment.

Having then seen that believers have no part in the resurrection of judgment, we have still to enquire, When will they appear before the judgment-seat of Christ? The answer is clear from many passages that it is on His return, and therefore consequent upon the first resurrection. This is the distinct teaching of the parables in Matthew xxv. 14, etc.; Luke xix. 11, etc. In the former, we have the words, "After a long time the lord of those servants cometh, and reckoneth with them" (Matt. xxv. 19); in the latter, the charge on departure is, "Occupy till I come." (Luke xix. 13.) In all the exhortations, too, addressed to the disciples, under responsibilty as servants, the coming of Christ is the goal to which they are directed to look; so also in the epistles (as, for example, 1 Cor. i. 7, 8; 1 Thess. i. 9, 10; iii. 12, 13; 2 Thess. i. ; 1 Timothy vi. 13-16; Titus ii. 11-14, etc.)

(β) We may, then, now answer our second question—For what purpose will believers appear before the judgment-seat of Christ? We have seen that it is not to be judged for sin; for the possession of everlasting life exempts them from this, and the judgment, due both to their sins and sinful condition, has already been borne by their Surety in His death. It is "that every one may receive the things [done] in [his] body;" and thus for the believer it is a judgment of his works or service. This truth cannot be too earnestly pressed upon our hearts and consciences; for it will stimulate us both to fidelity and zeal to remember that we must "be manifested" (as the word is) before the judgment-seat of Christ. Let it be remembered, however, that before we are thus judged we are already raised, and made like unto our Lord (Phil. iii. 20, 21 ; 1 John iii. 2), bodily as well as spiritually; and hence that we shall have full fellowship with Him in His judgment upon our works. Still it is a very solemn consideration, that in regard to those things which we now excuse or allow to pass unjudged, we shall then take part with Christ in condemning as unworthy of Him whom we professed to serve; as traces of Egypt which ought to have been judged and rolled away; as actings of the flesh which God in His infinite mercy and grace had put into the place of death, and which He has given us power to keep there through the indwelling Spirit. Hence the blessing of constant and faithful self-judgment, as even now in spirit manifested before the judgment-seat of Christ. May we be enabled to do this, and may "the very God of peace sanctify you wholly; and your whole spirit, soul, and body be preserved blameless unto the coming of our Lord Jesus Christ." (1 Thess. v. 23.)

3. The final judgment of the wicked will take place at the end of the millennium. Earth has been, and will yet be, the scene of many a judgment of the living; and so also "when the Son of man comes in His glory, and all the holy angels with Him, then shall He sit upon the throne of His glory: and before Him shall be gathered all nations," etc. (Matt. xxv. 31, etc.) This judgment scene is often confounded with that which takes place before the great white throne; but it is entirely distinct. It is, as the word declares, the judgment of the nations, living nations at

the coming of the Son of man in glory; a judgment therefore preparatory to His sway from the river unto the ends of the earth. The final judgment, that of the dead, is found in the Revelation, and is thus described: "And I saw the dead, small and great, stand before God" (it should be, before the throne); "and the books were opened: and another book was opened, which is [the book] of life: and the dead were judged out of those things which were written in the books, according to their works. And the sea gave up the dead which were in it; and death and hell (rather, hades) delivered up the dead which were in them: and they were judged every man according to their works. And death and hell were cast into the lake of fire. This is the second death. And whosoever was not found written in the book of life was cast into the lake of fire." (Rev. xx. 11–15.)

This is the "resurrection of judgment" of which our Lord speaks in the gospel of John; and will include therefore all the unsaved, and the unsaved alone. True that the book of life is there; but there is no indication of any saints to be judged. The book of life is opened to show that the names of those to be judged were *not* there; and thus they are condemned on both negative and positive grounds. Their names were not written in the book of life, and their works declared them amenable to righteous judgment, and they thus fall hopelessly under the everlasting sentence of the lake of fire, which is the second death, a sentence from which there is no appeal and no escape.

Are any of my readers still unsaved? Let me beseech you to ponder upon this solemn scene. He who sits upon that great white throne as the Judge is the Blessed One who, now seated in the glory at the right hand of God, is proclaimed to you as a Saviour. Concerning Him the divine decree has gone forth, "That at the name of Jesus every knee should bow, of [things] in heaven, and [things] in earth, and [things] under the earth" (*i.e.* celestial, terrestrial, and infernal beings); "and [that] every tongue should confess that Jesus Christ is Lord, to the glory of God the Father." (Phil. ii. 10, 11.) None therefore can escape; but the question which affects you, and will affect you eternally, is whether you will bow the knee to Him now while it is the accepted time, and the day of salvation, or whether you will be constrained to bow before Him as your Judge on the throne. Bow before Him now, in self-judgment, taking the place of a sinner, and looking to Him as the Saviour, the Lamb of God which taketh away the sin of the world, and you will not come into judgment, but will, while you look, pass from death unto life. Refusing Him as a Saviour, despising the grace of God which promises everlasting life to

THE JUDGMENT. 135

every one that believeth on Him, you will have to bow before and under the rod of His judgment, and at the same time to confess that He is Lord to the glory of God the Father. Awful alternative! Oh that even the contemplation of it may be used of the Lord to bring you, even as you read, as a lost sinner to His feet, so that finding Him as your Saviour, you may be amongst that happy number who are waiting for His return, and who will never stand before the great white throne.

> "Lamb of God, Thou now art seated
> High upon Thy Father's throne;
> All Thy gracious work completed,
> All Thy mighty vict'ry won:
> Every knee in heaven is bending
> To the Lamb for sinners slain;
> Every voice and harp is swelling,—
> Worthy is the Lamb to reign."

> "Unto Him who loved us—gave us
> Every pledge that love could give;
> Freely shed His blood to save us;
> Gave His life that we might live;
> Be the kingdom,
> And dominion,
> And the glory evermore!"

LONDON:
W. H. BROOM, 25, PATERNOSTER SQUARE.

www.ingramcontent.com/pod-product-compliance
Lightning Source LLC
Chambersburg PA
CBHW020108170426
43199CB00009B/443